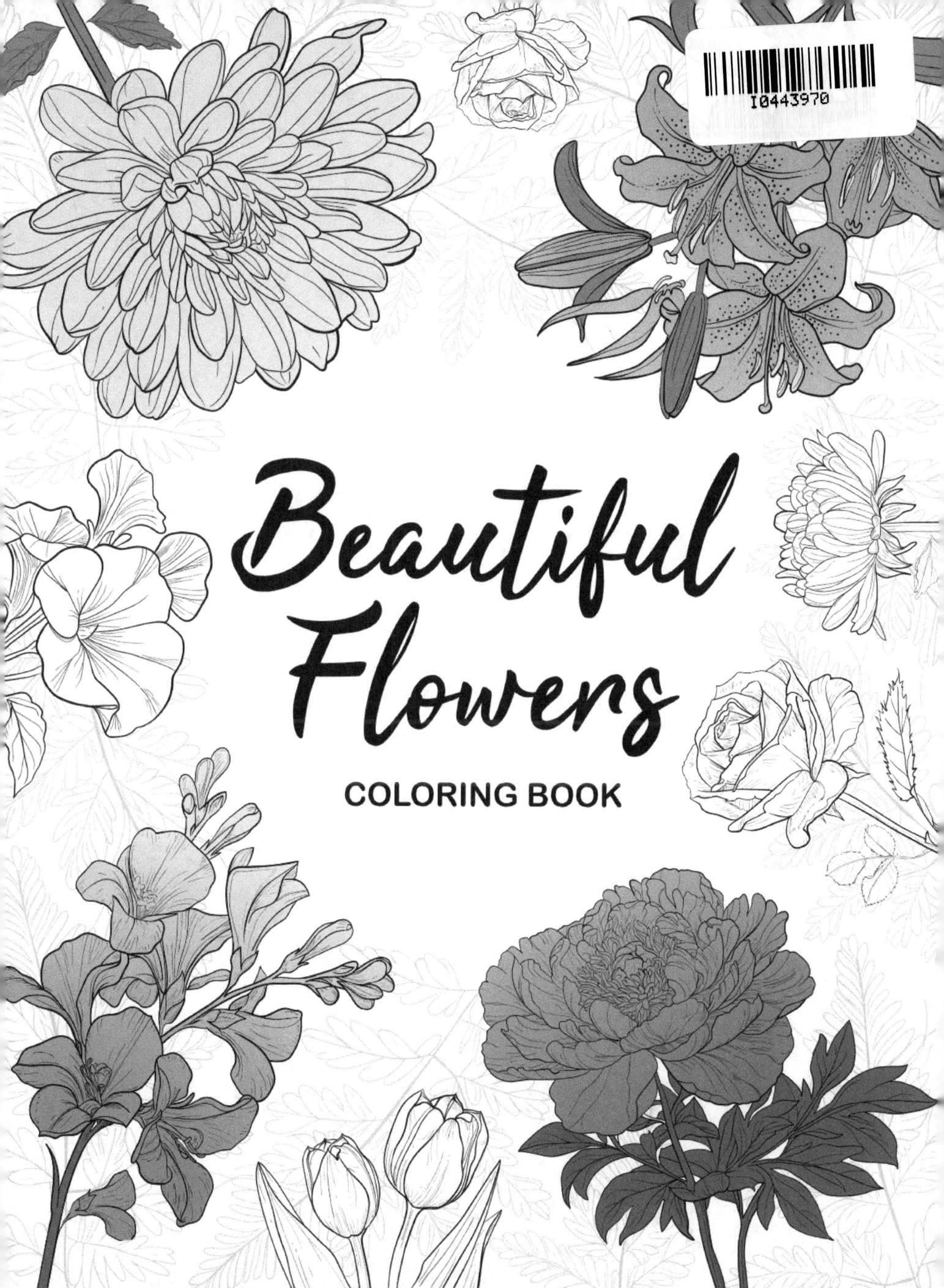

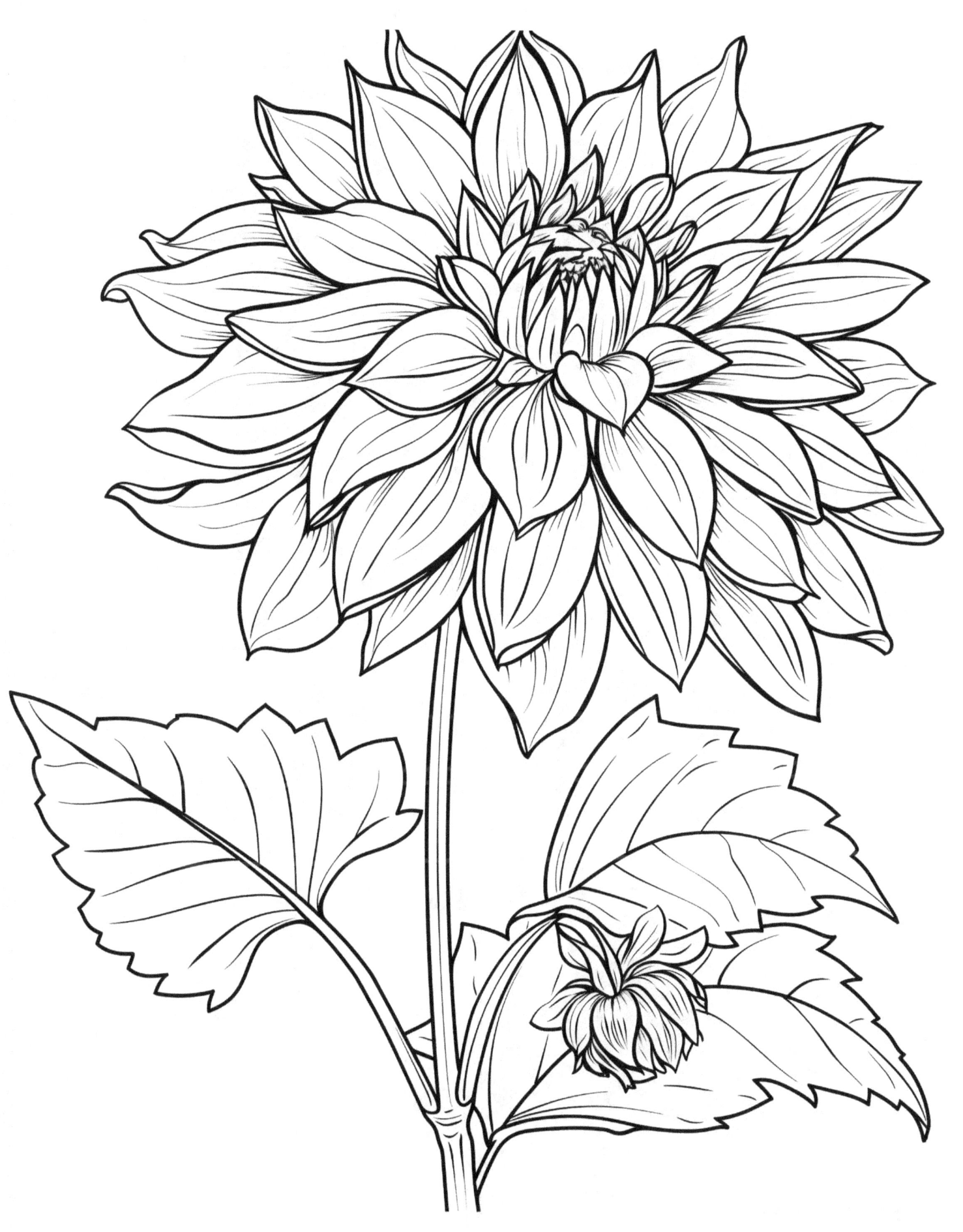

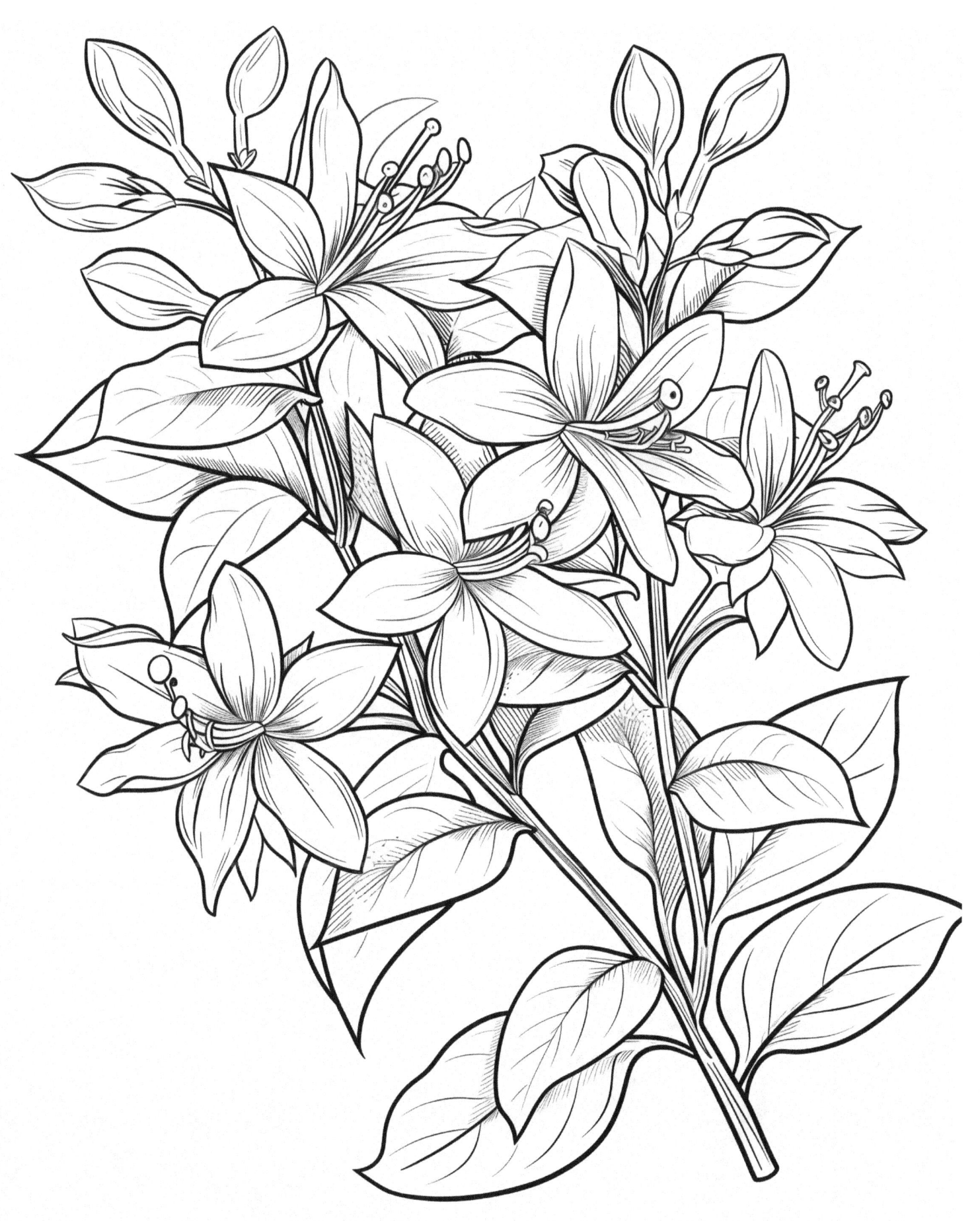

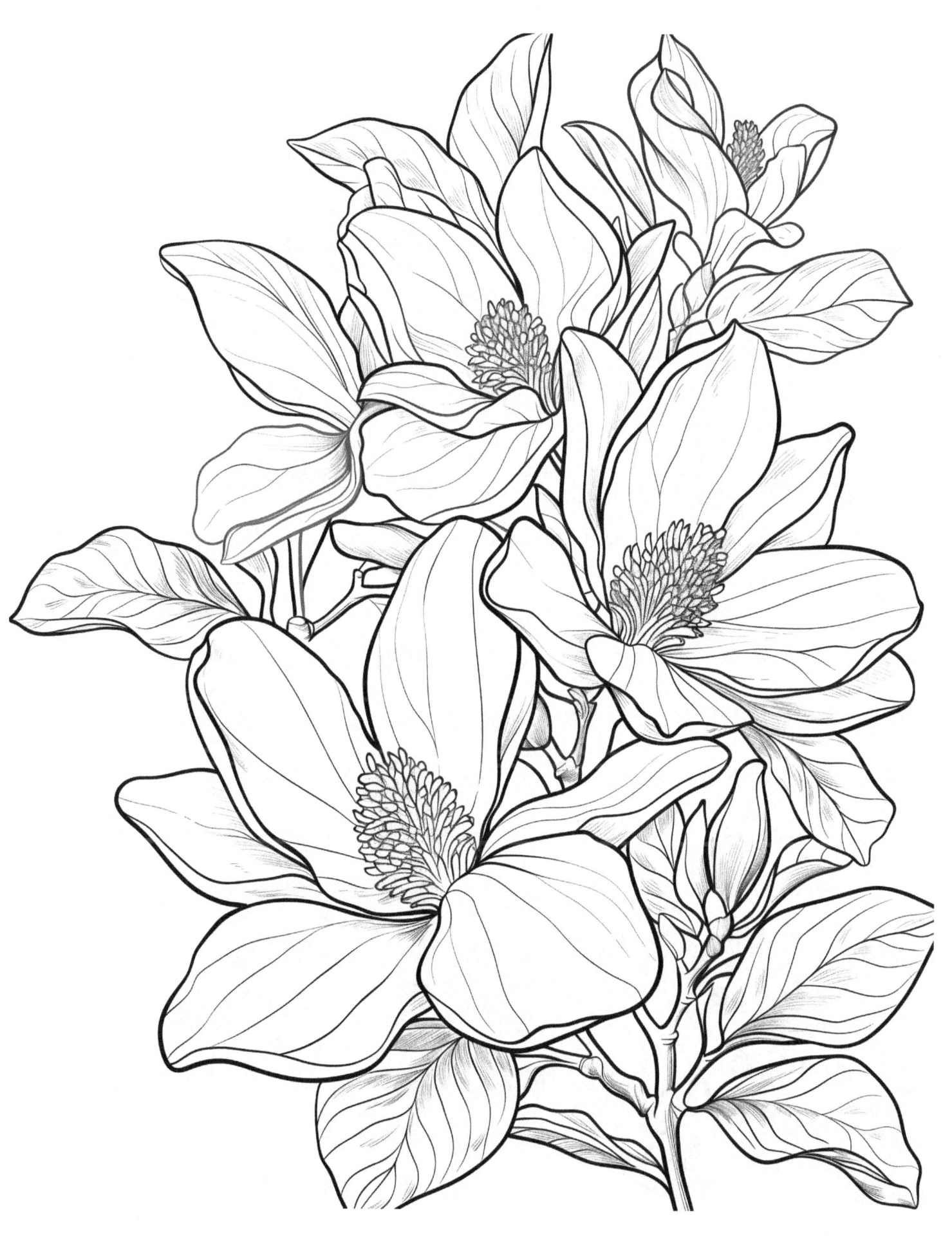

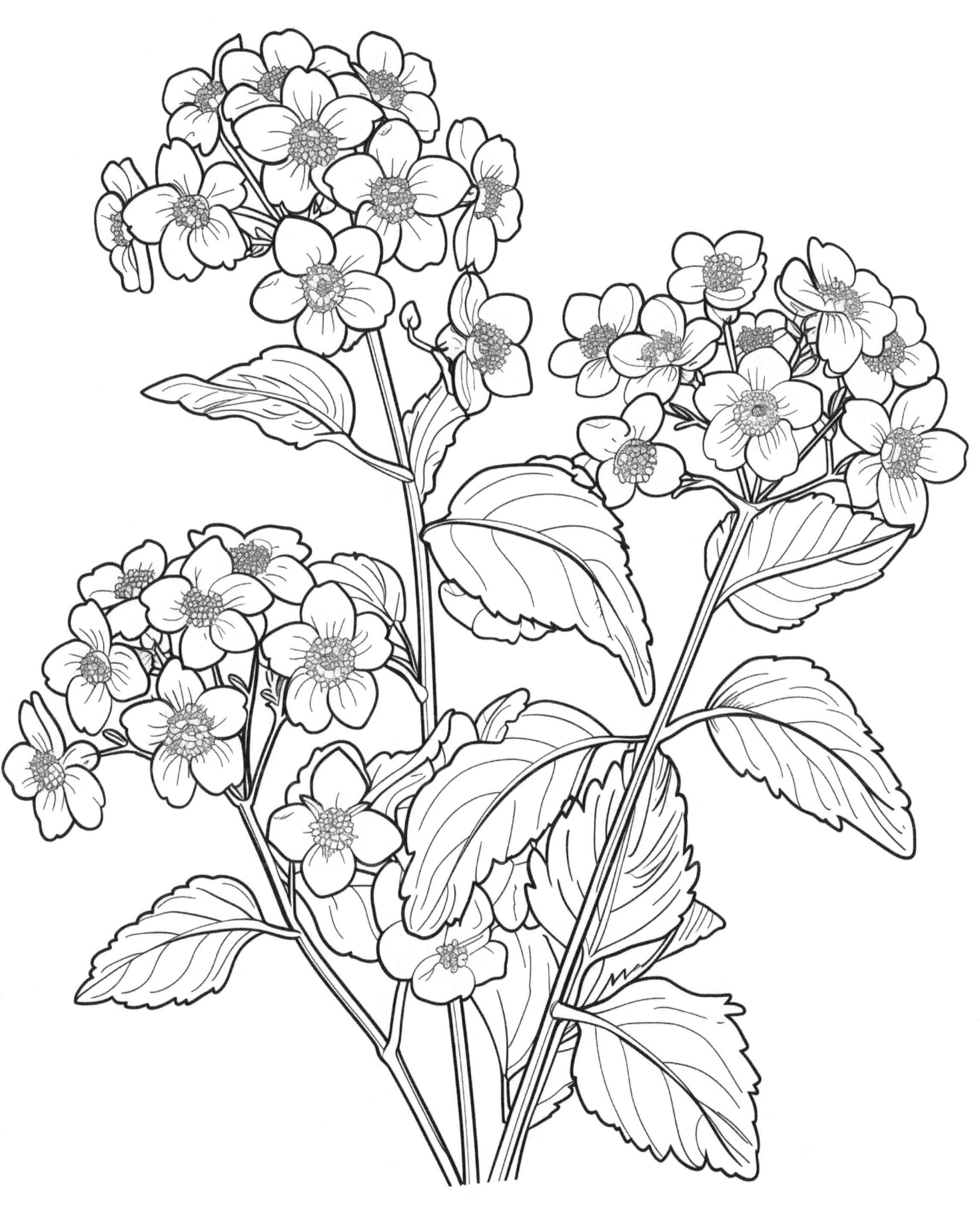

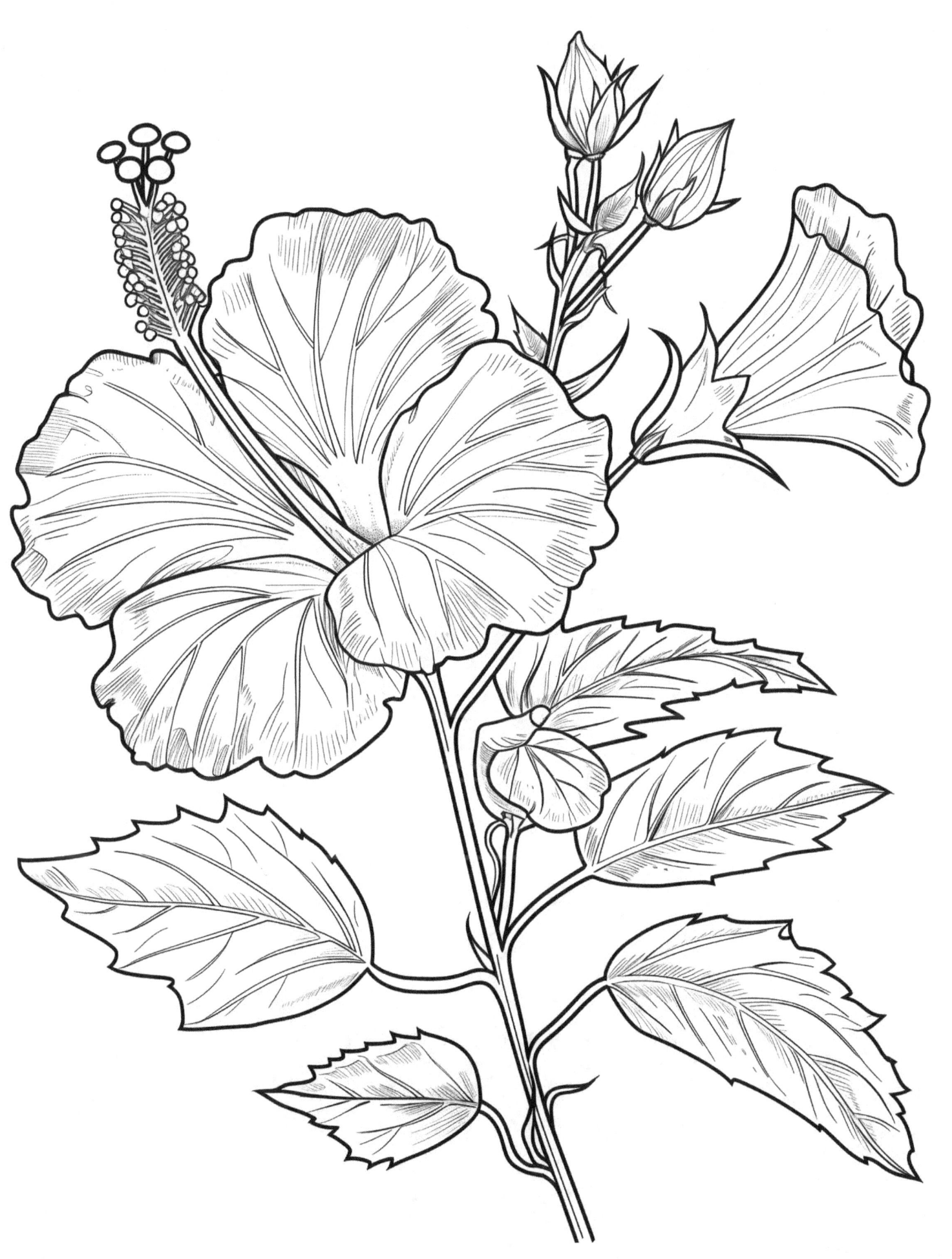

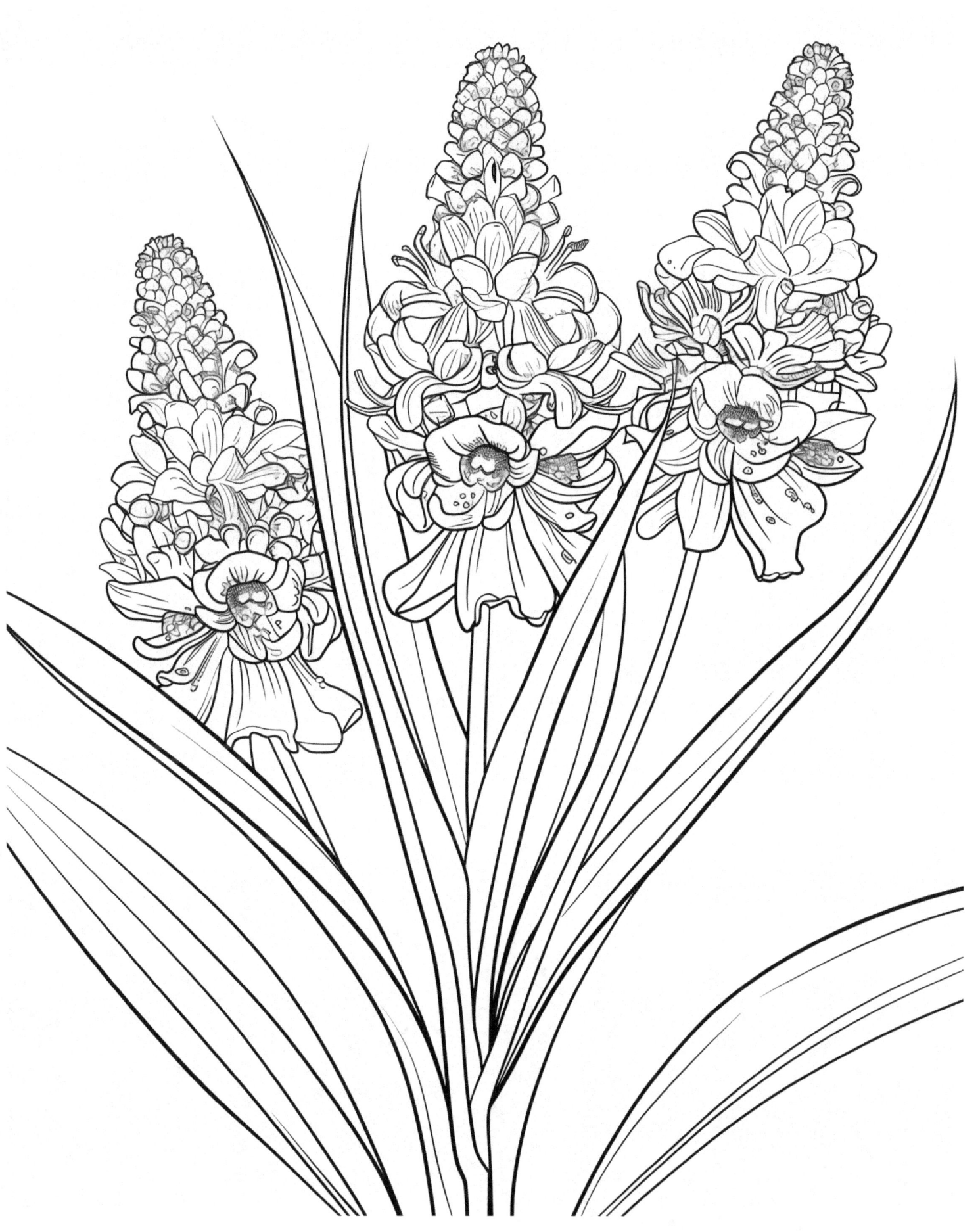

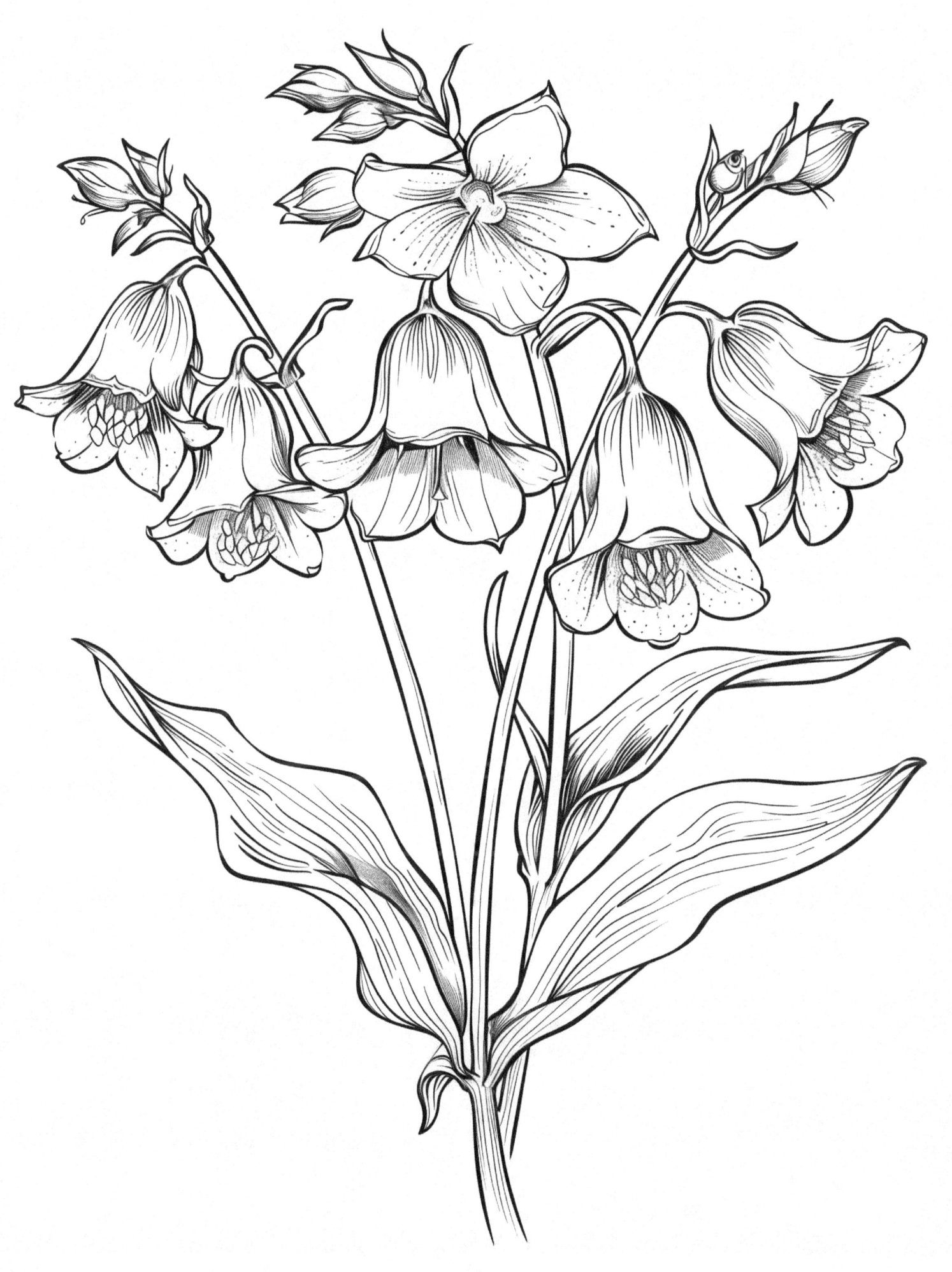

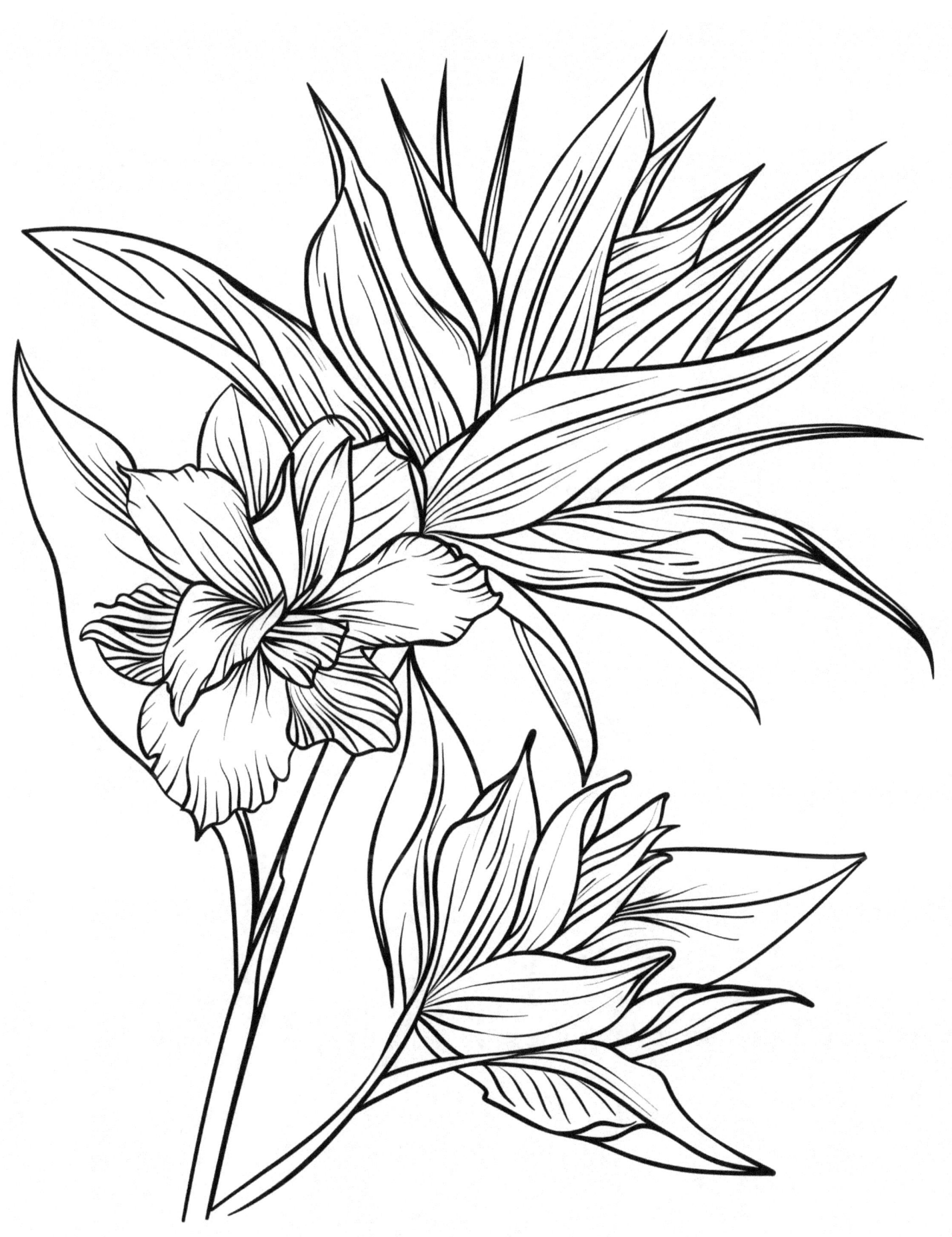

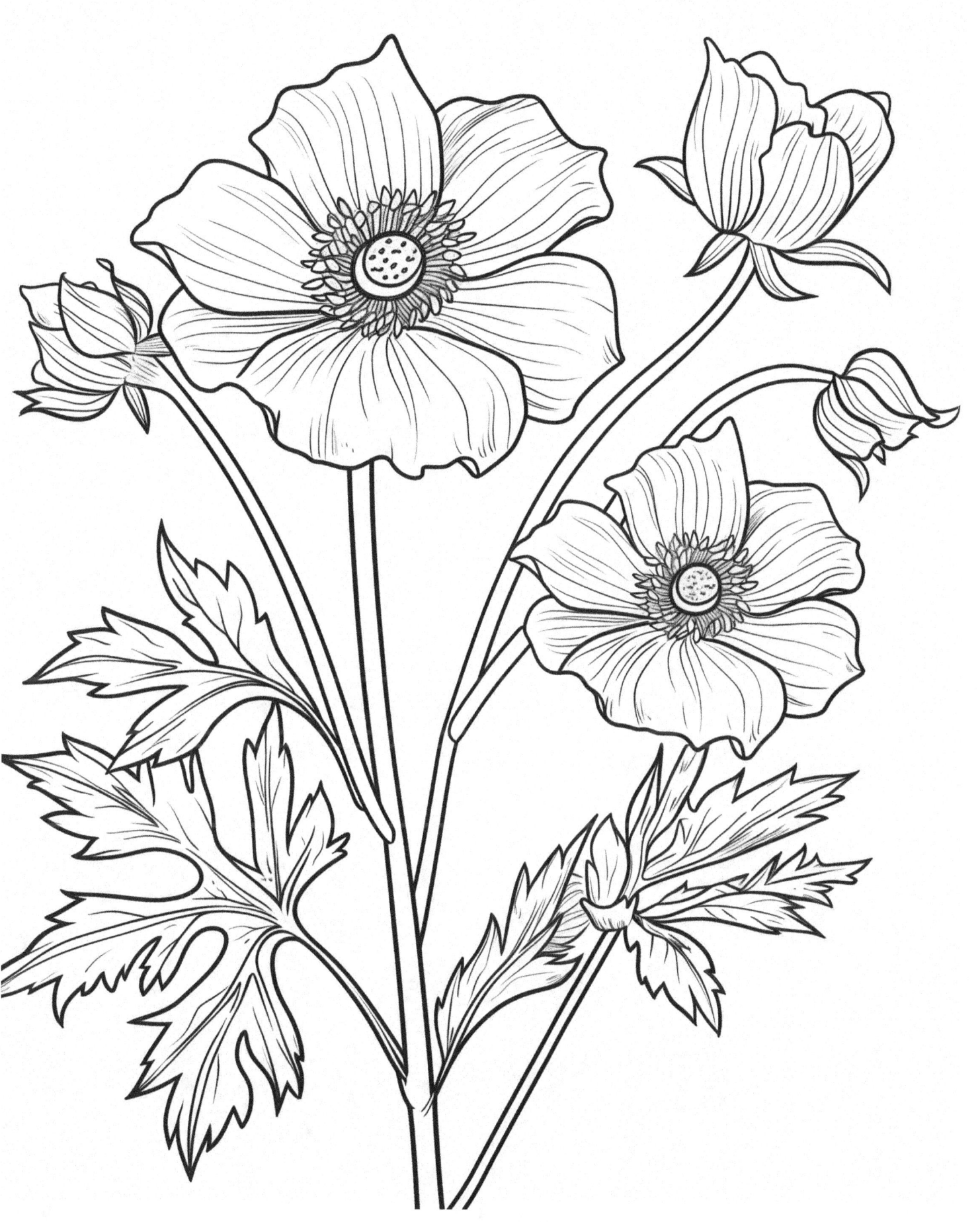

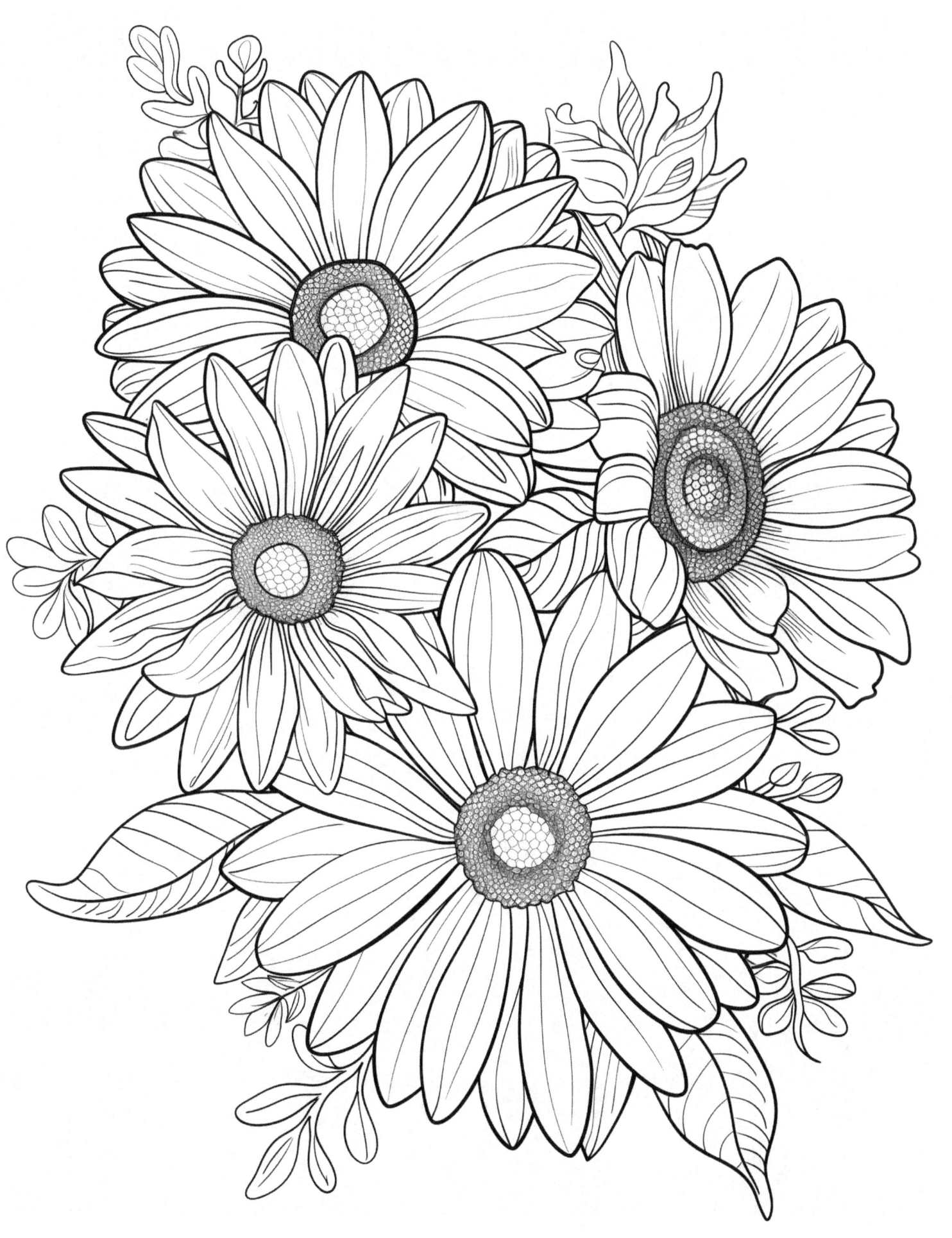

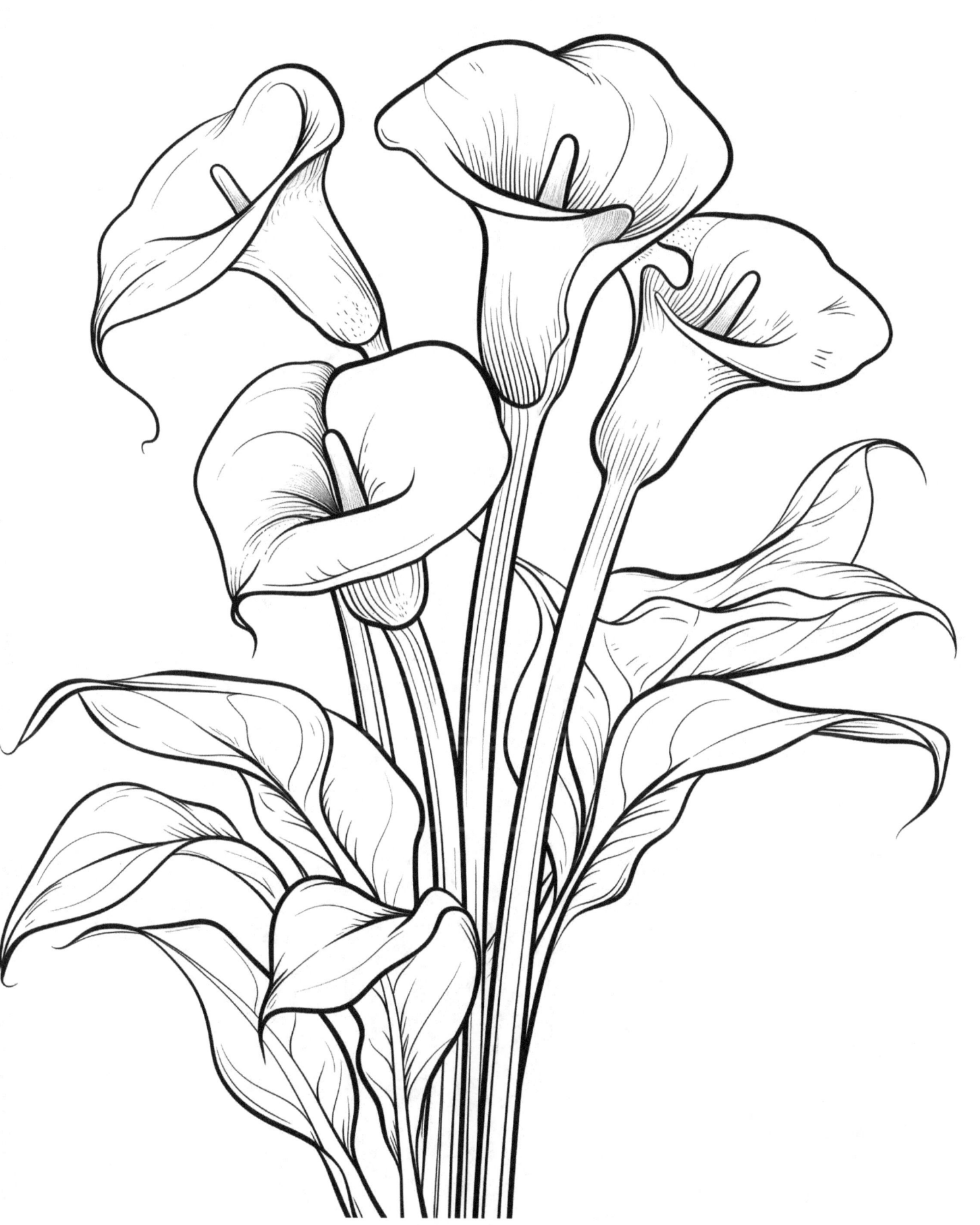

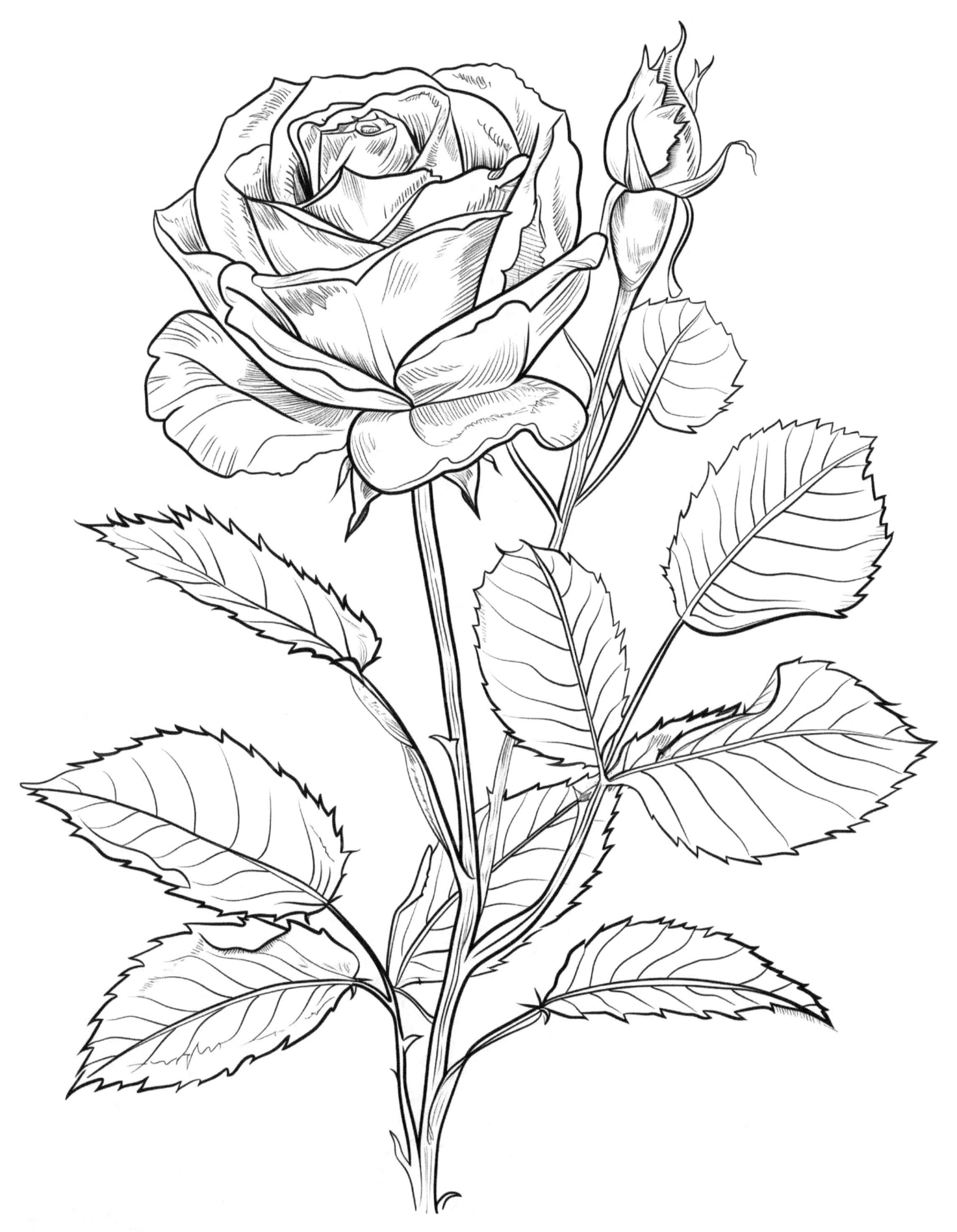

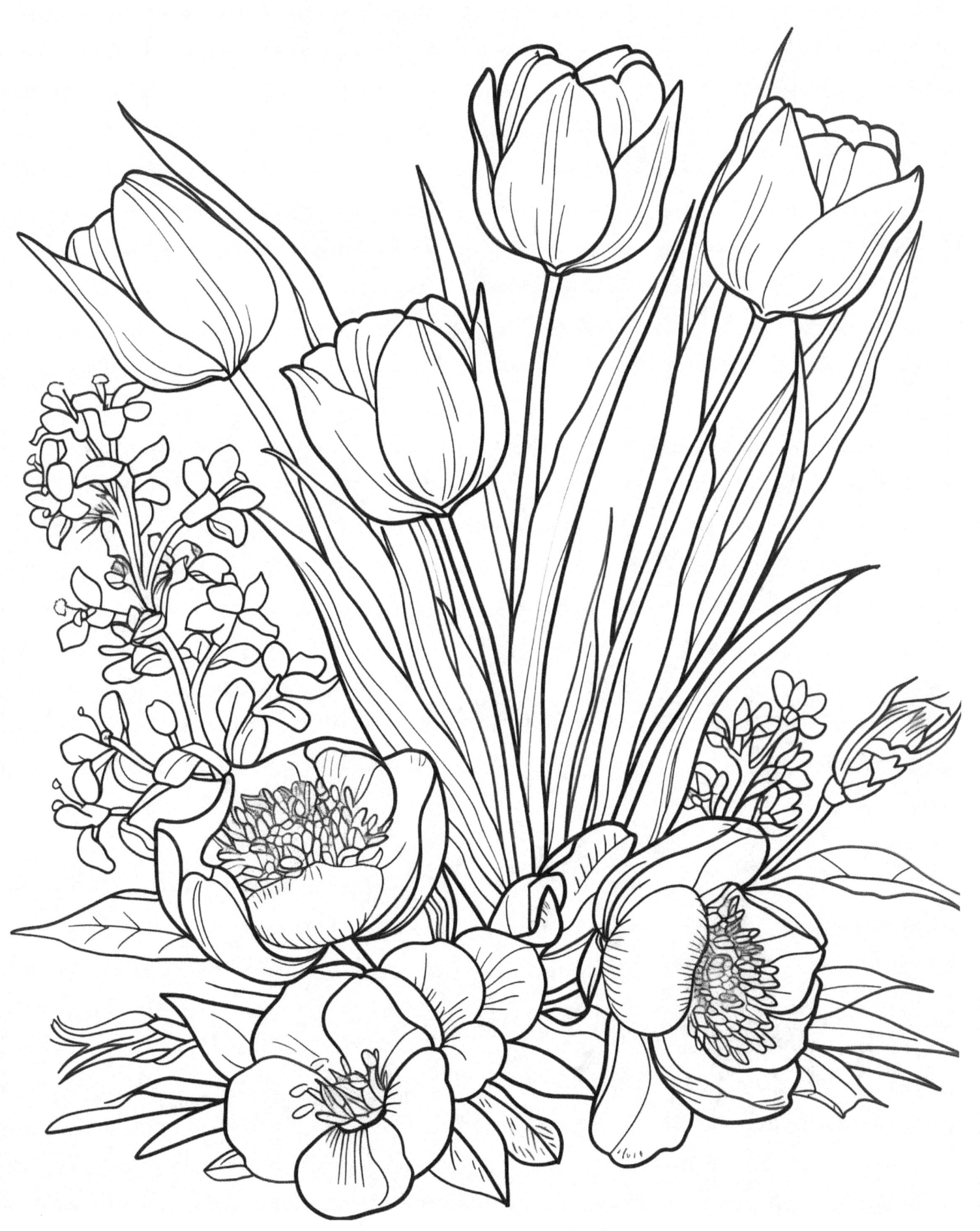

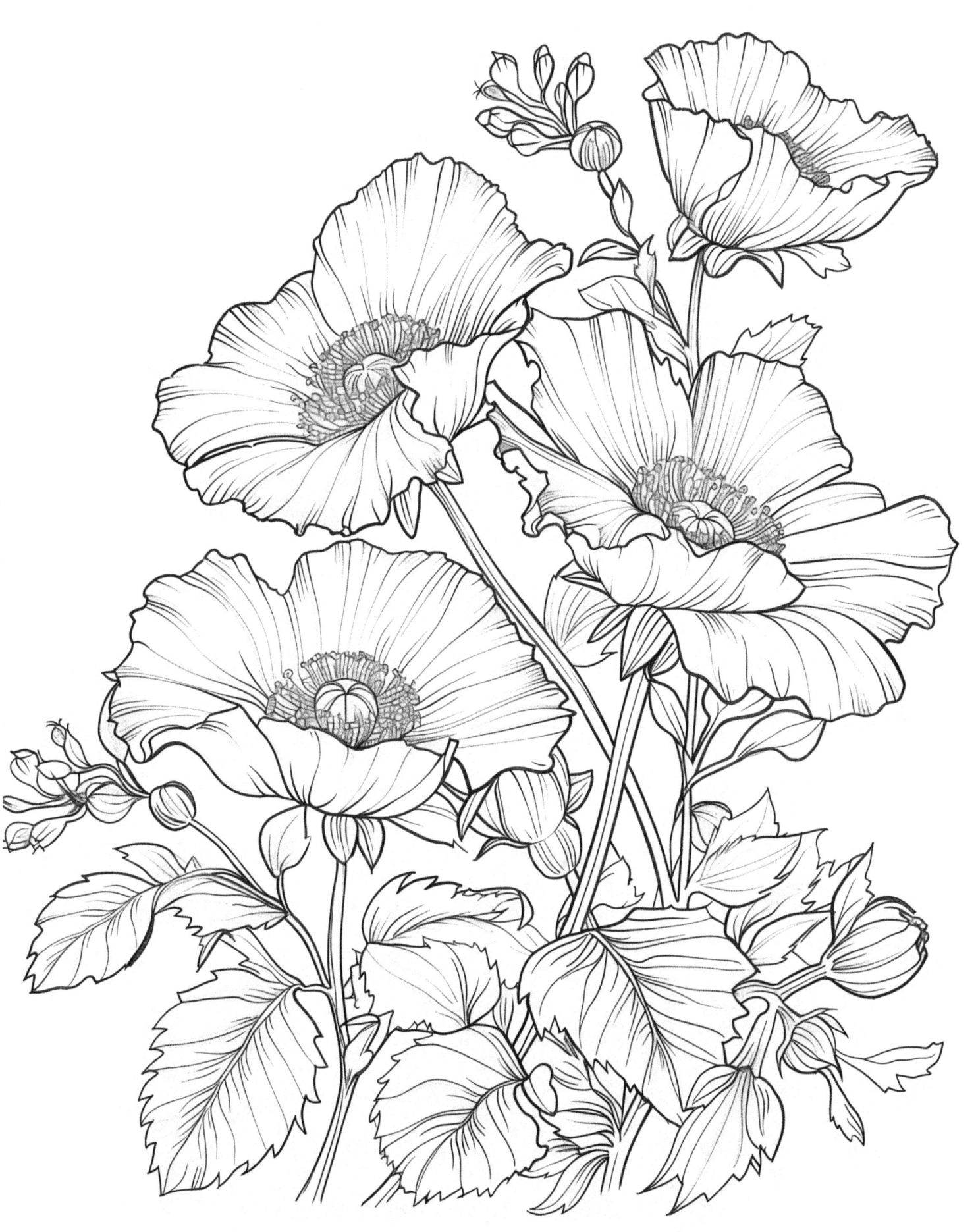

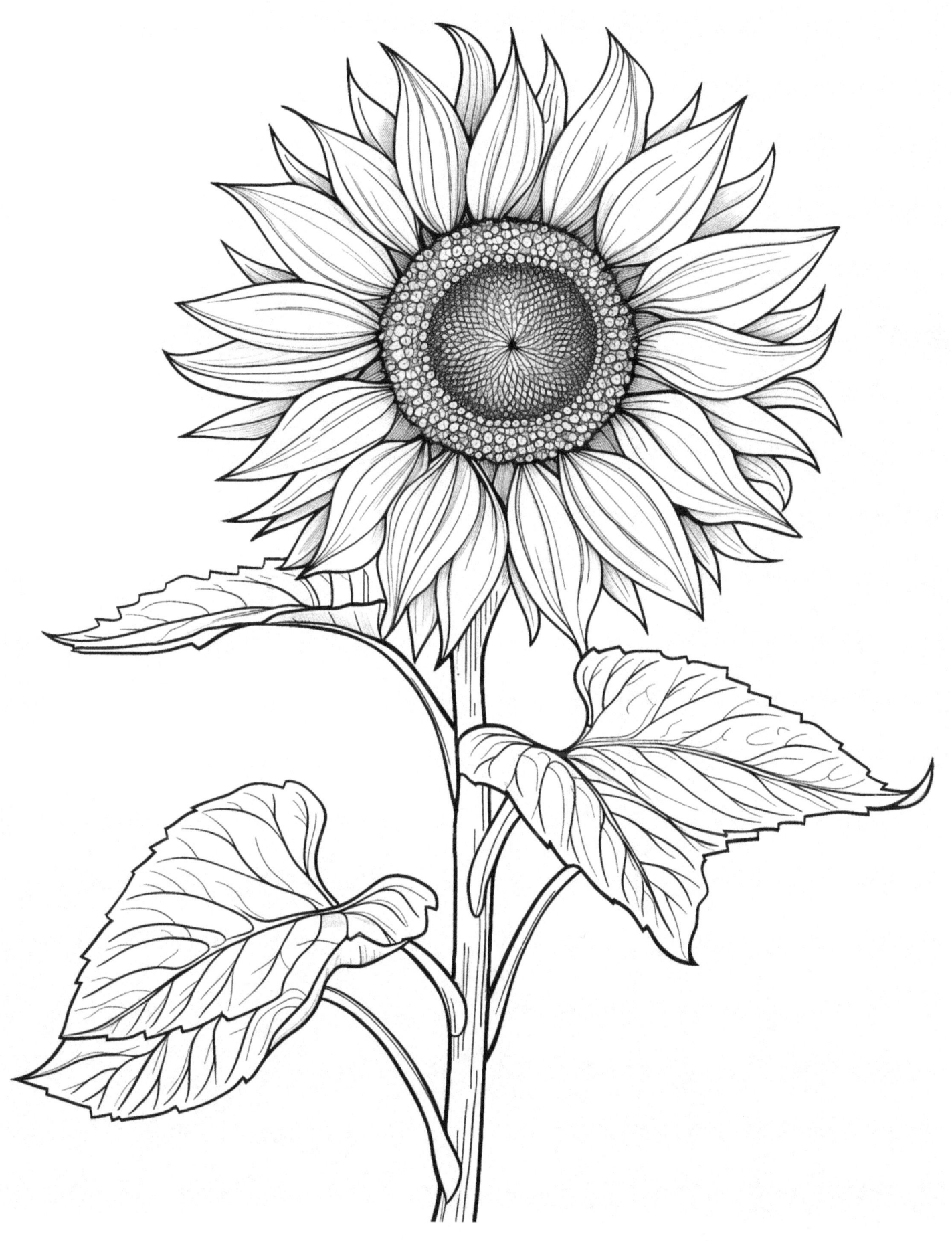

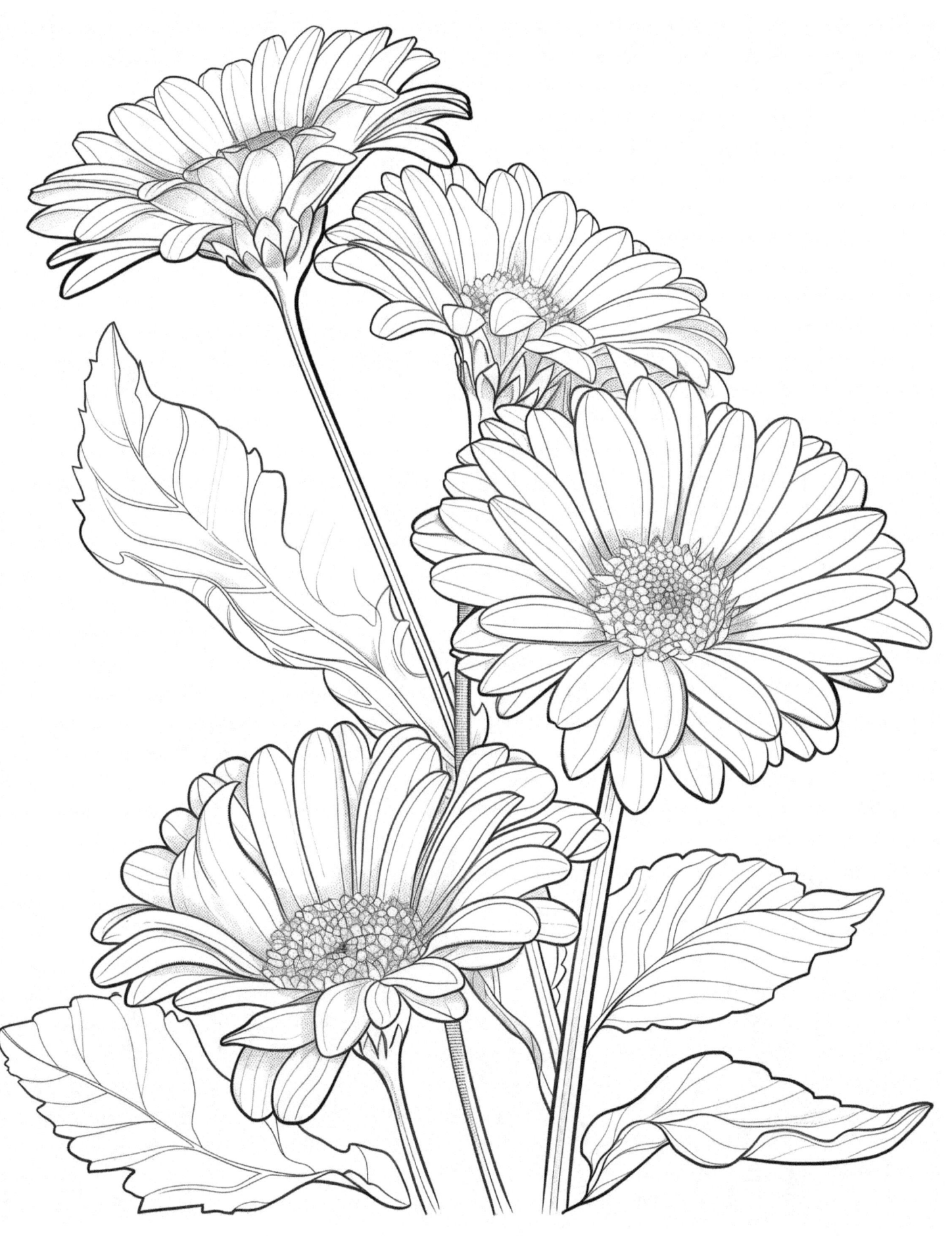

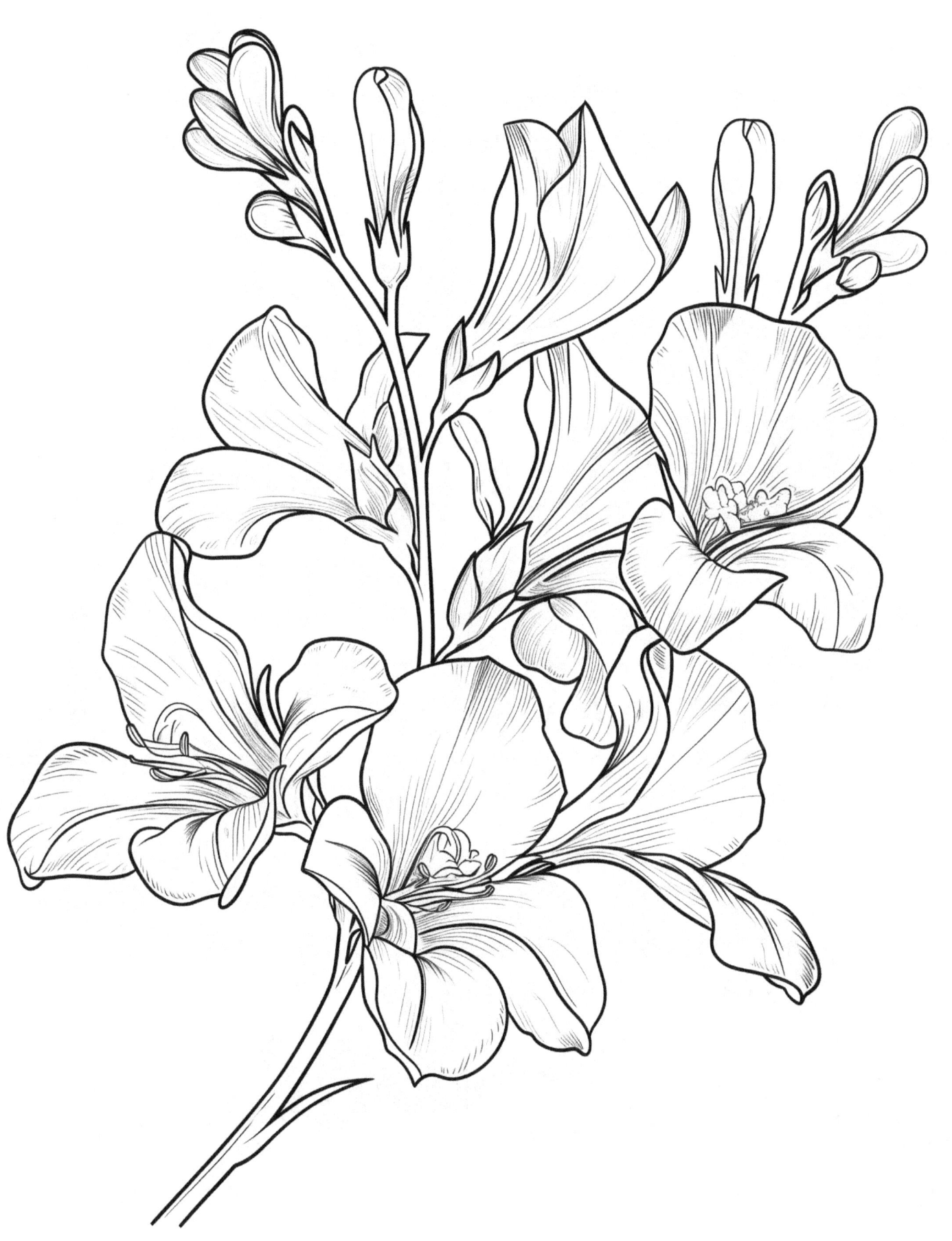

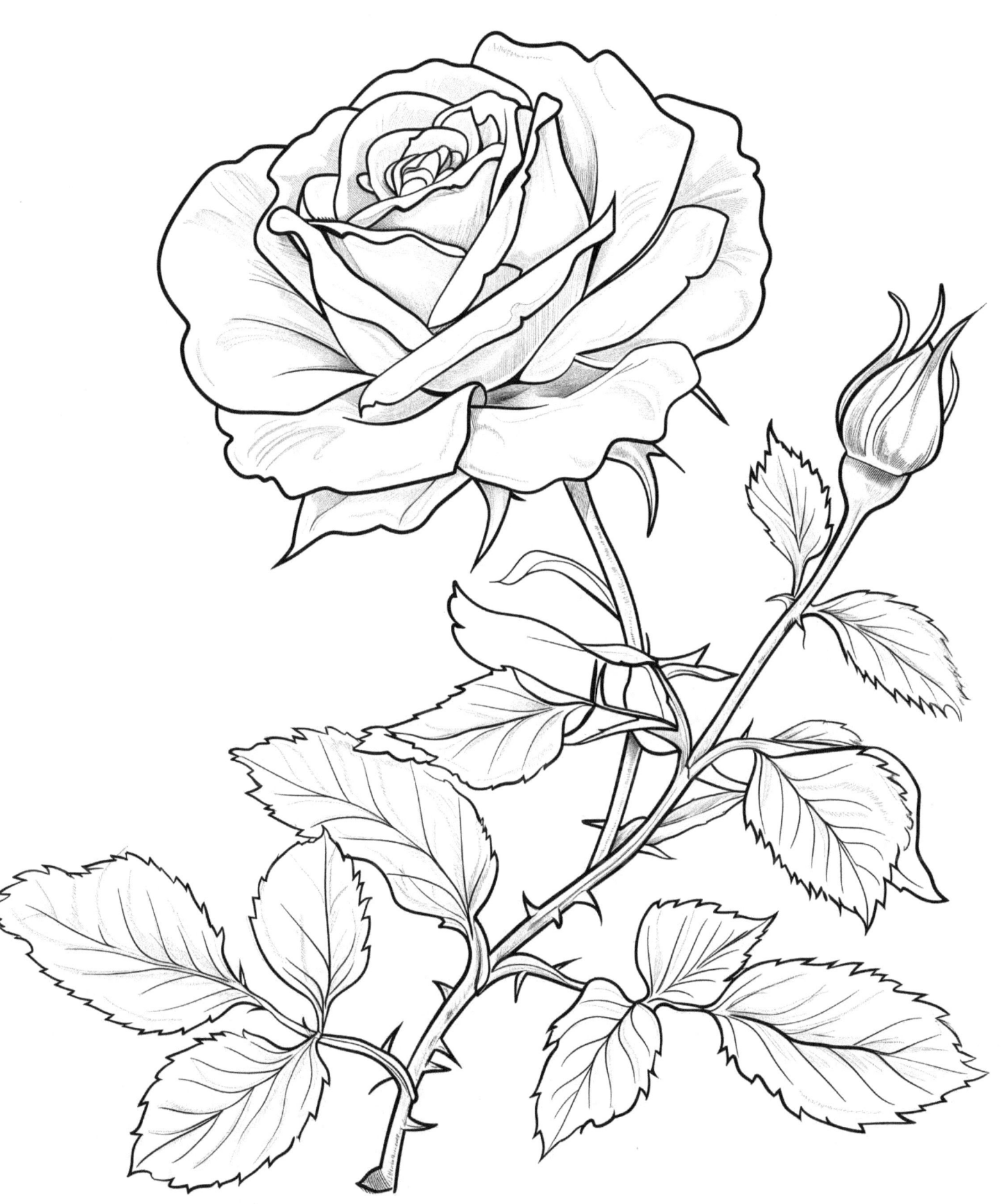

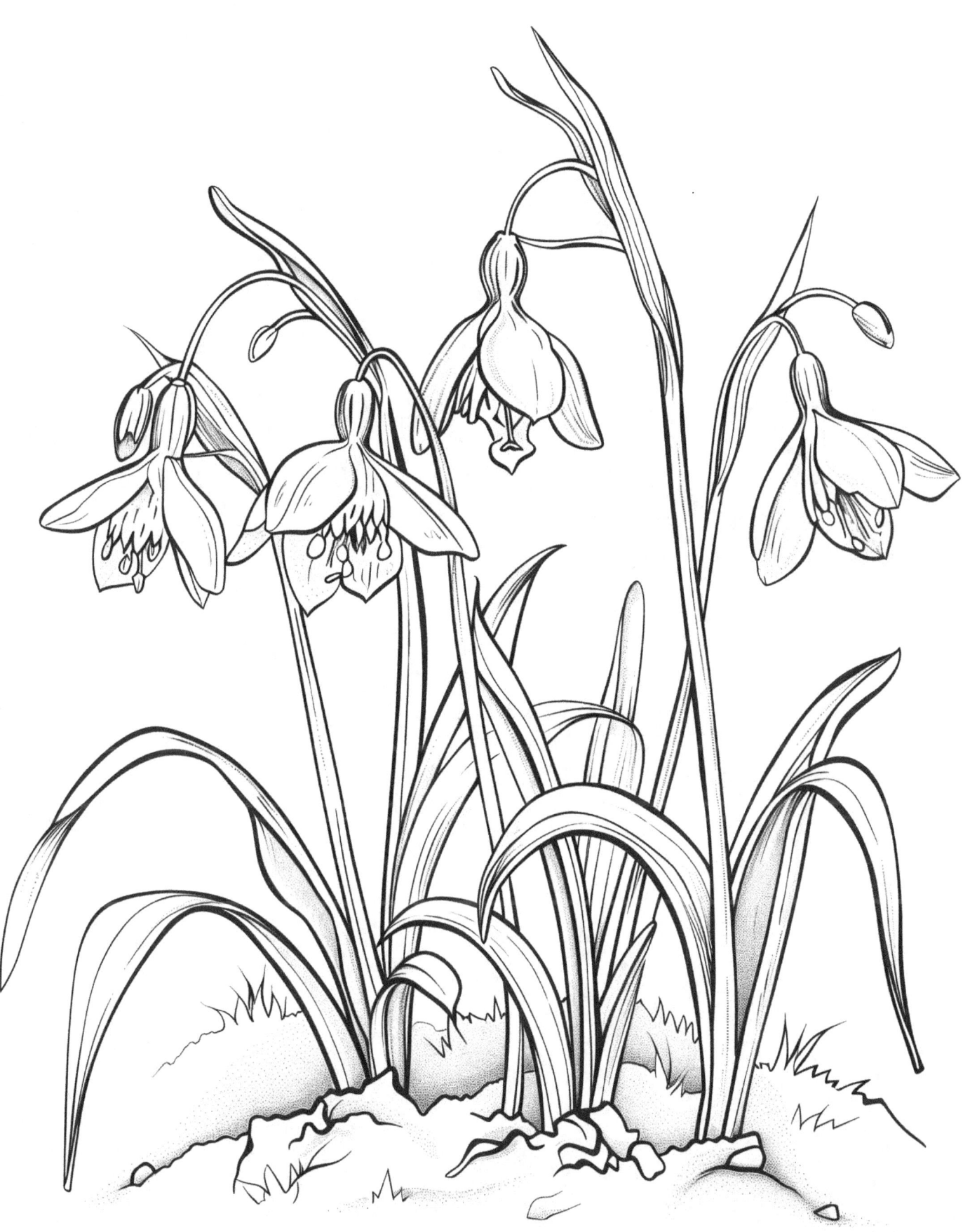

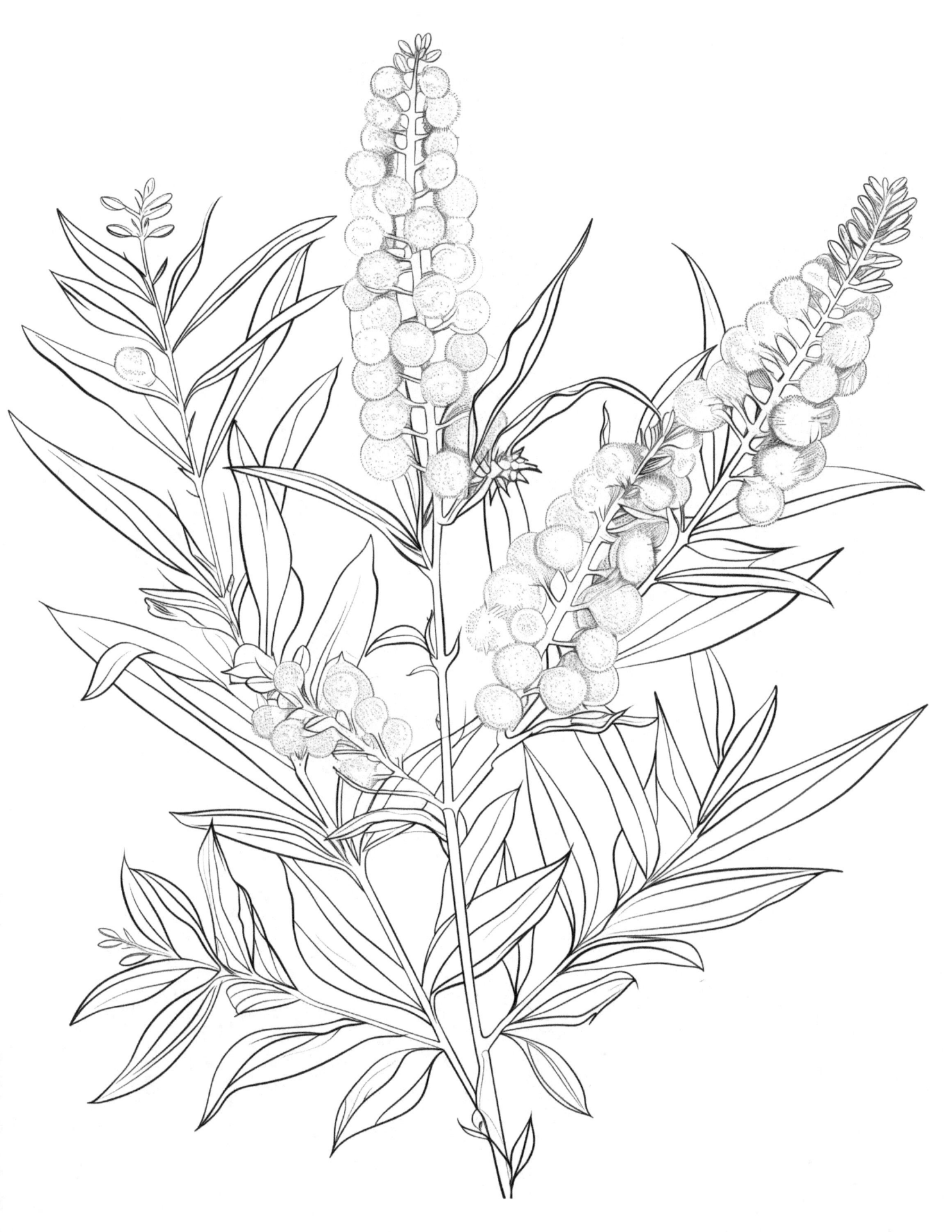

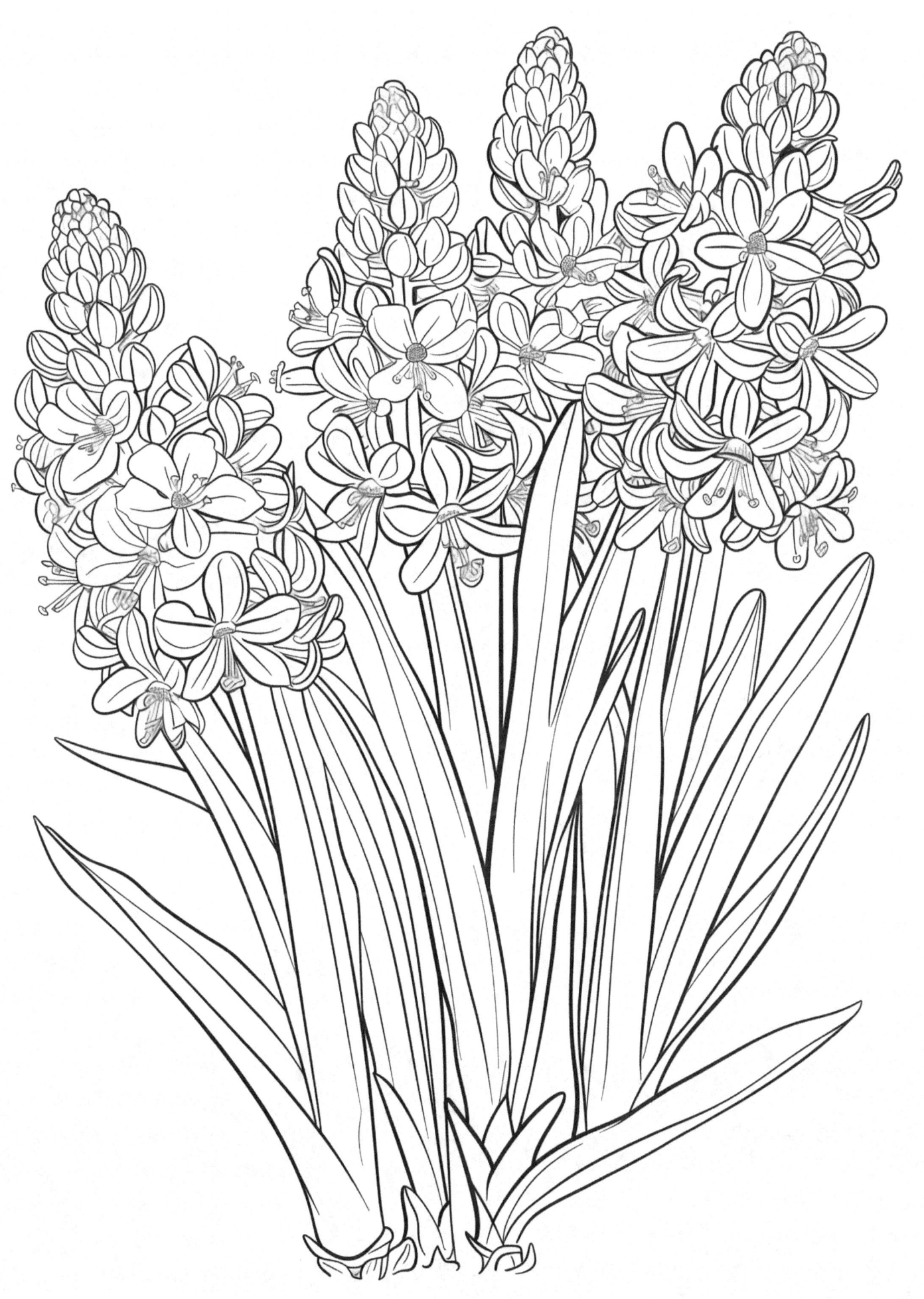

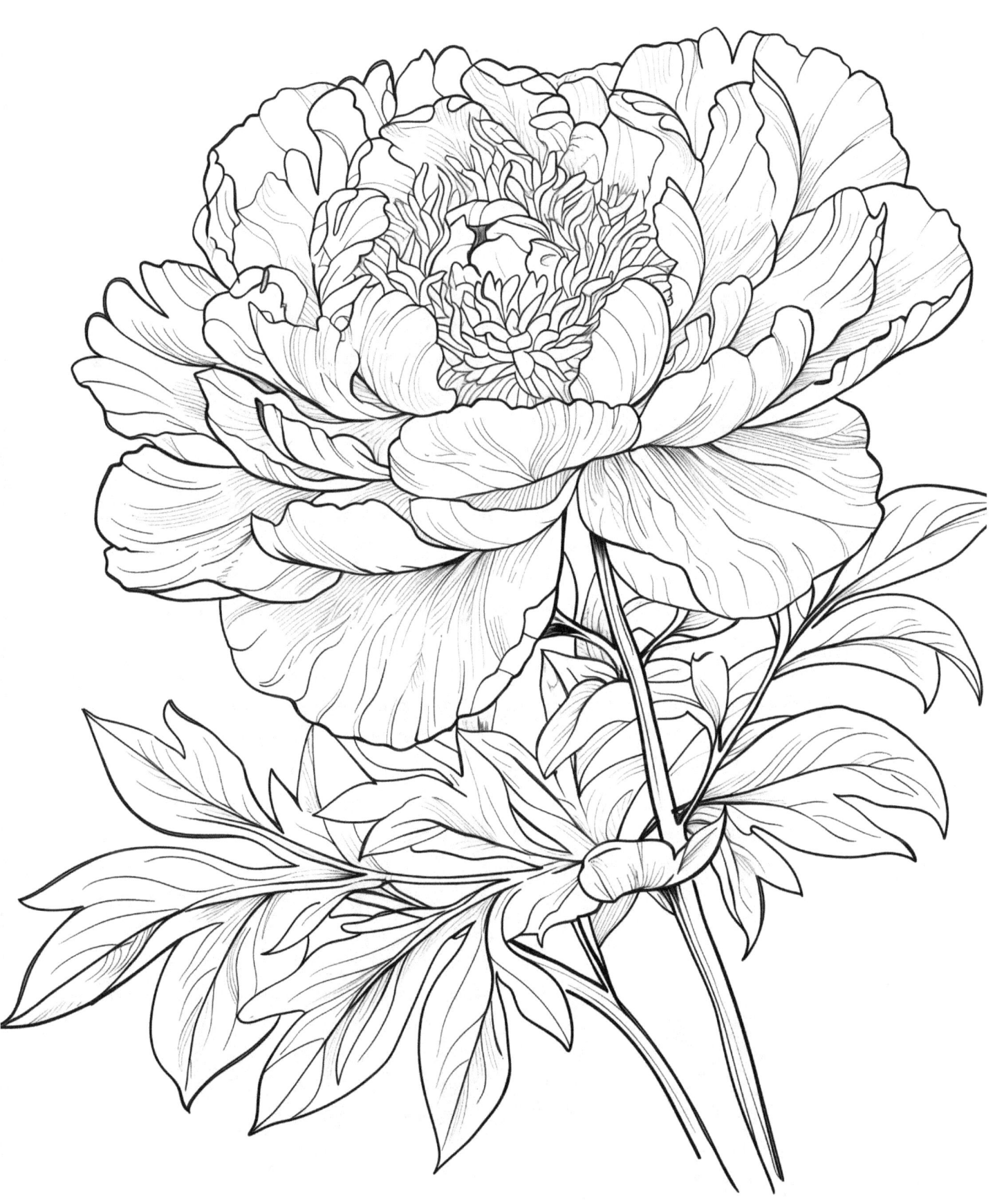

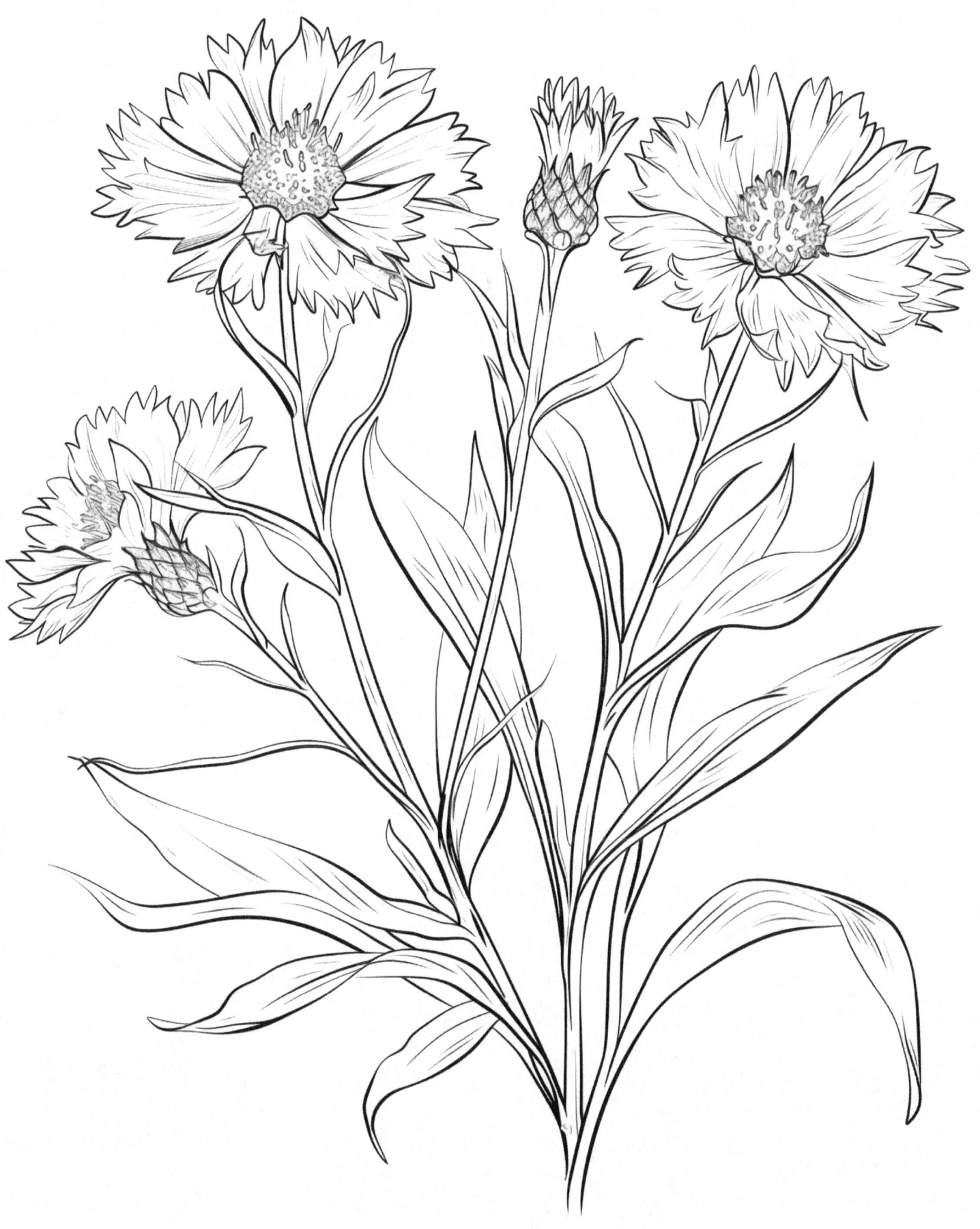

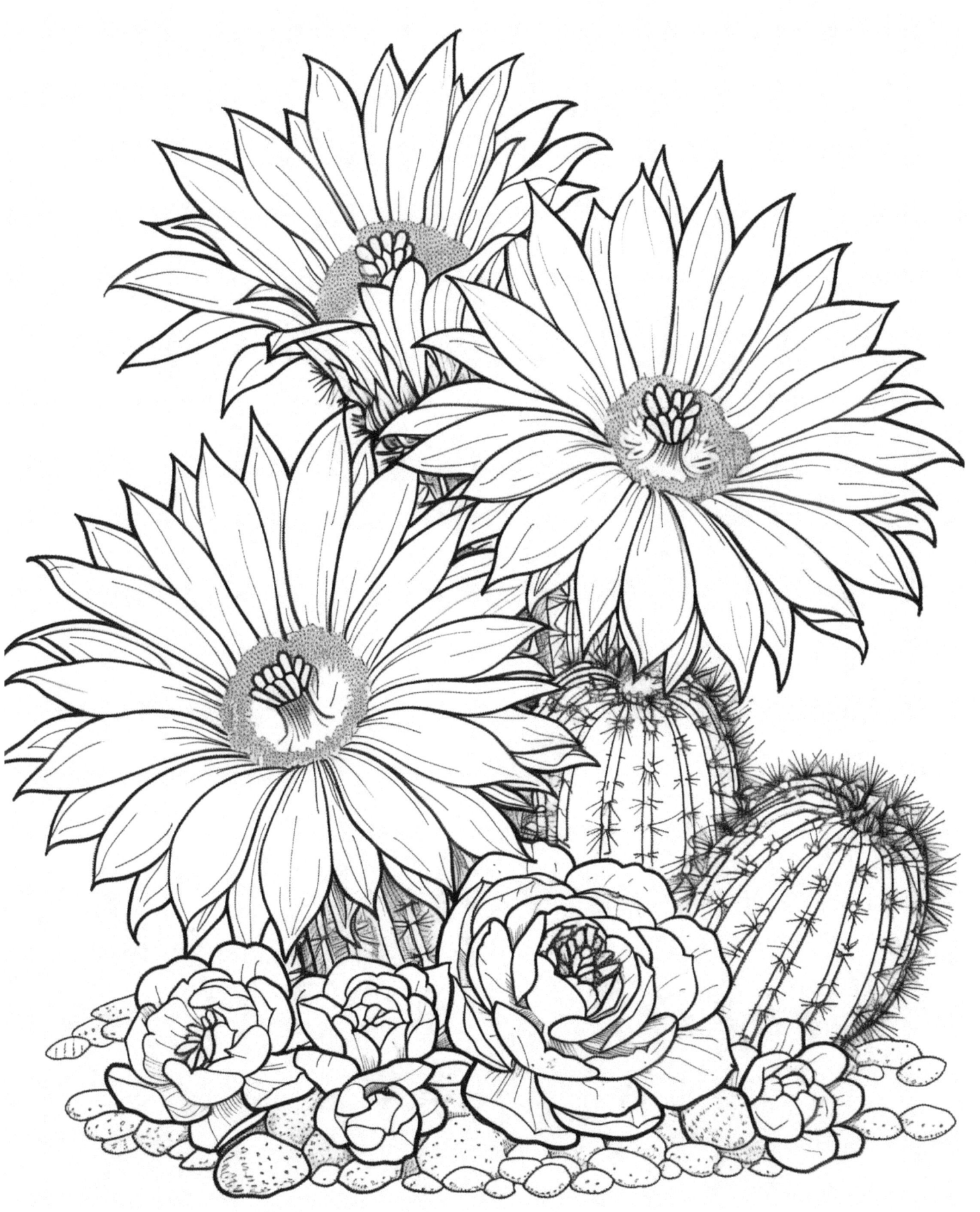

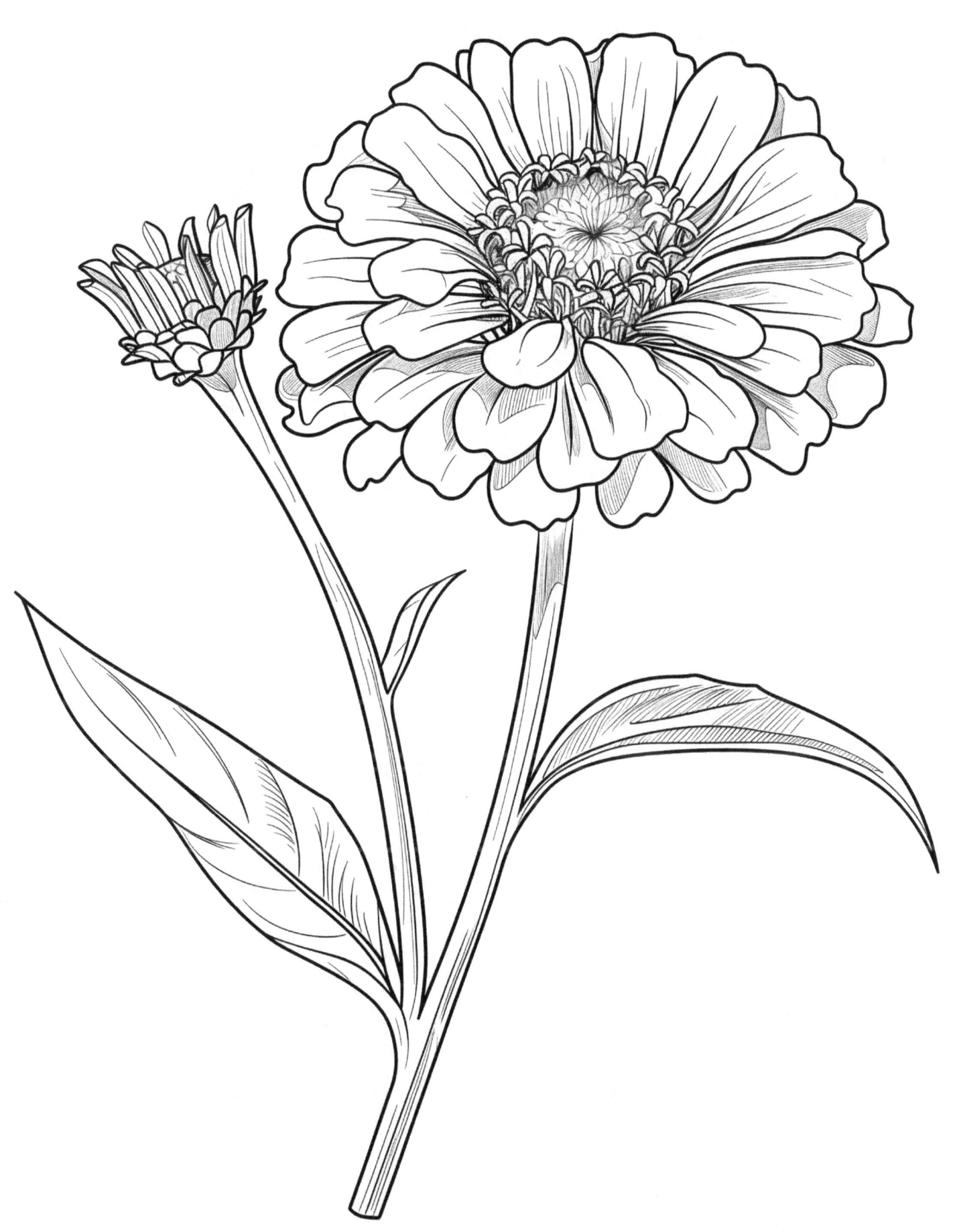

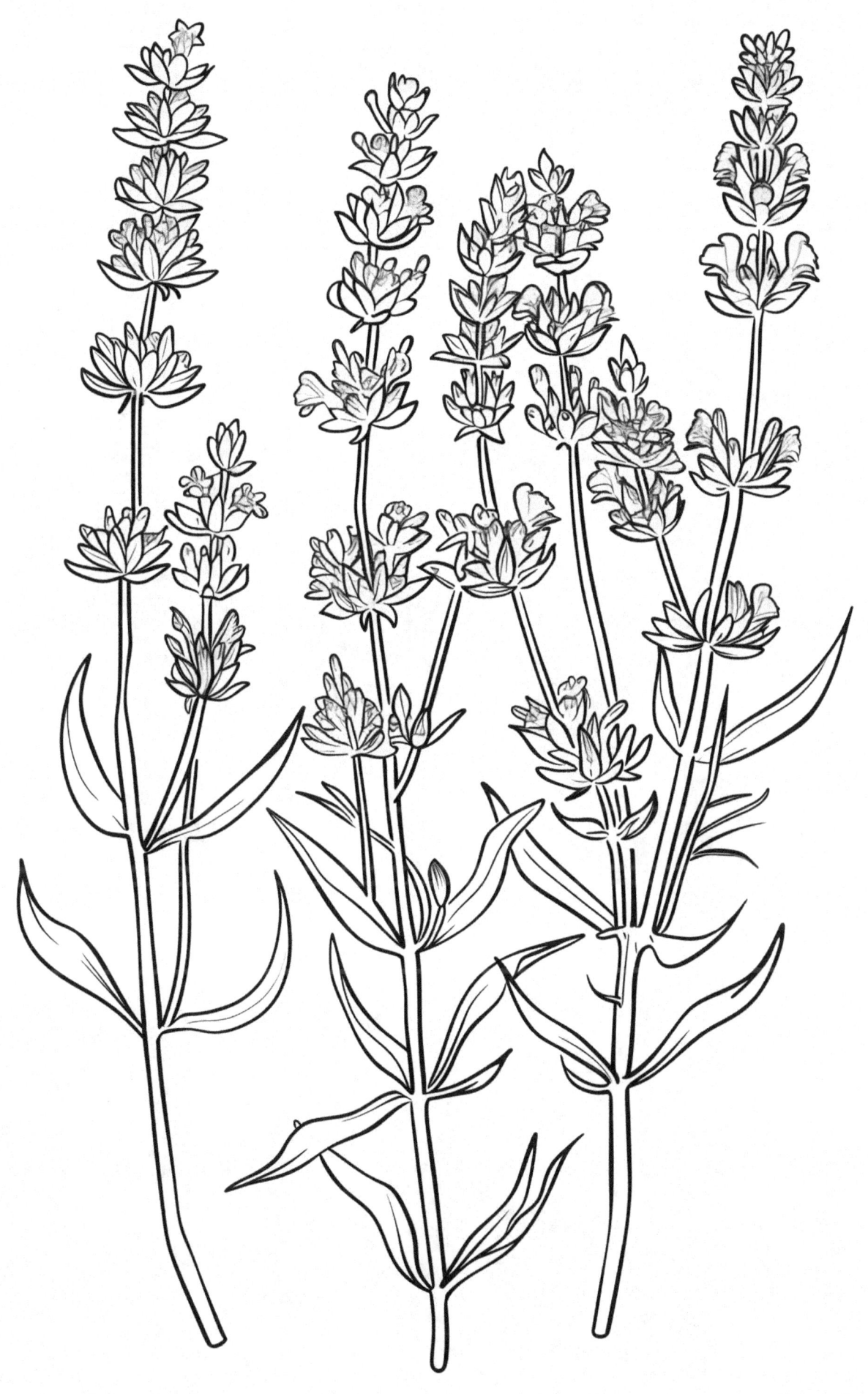

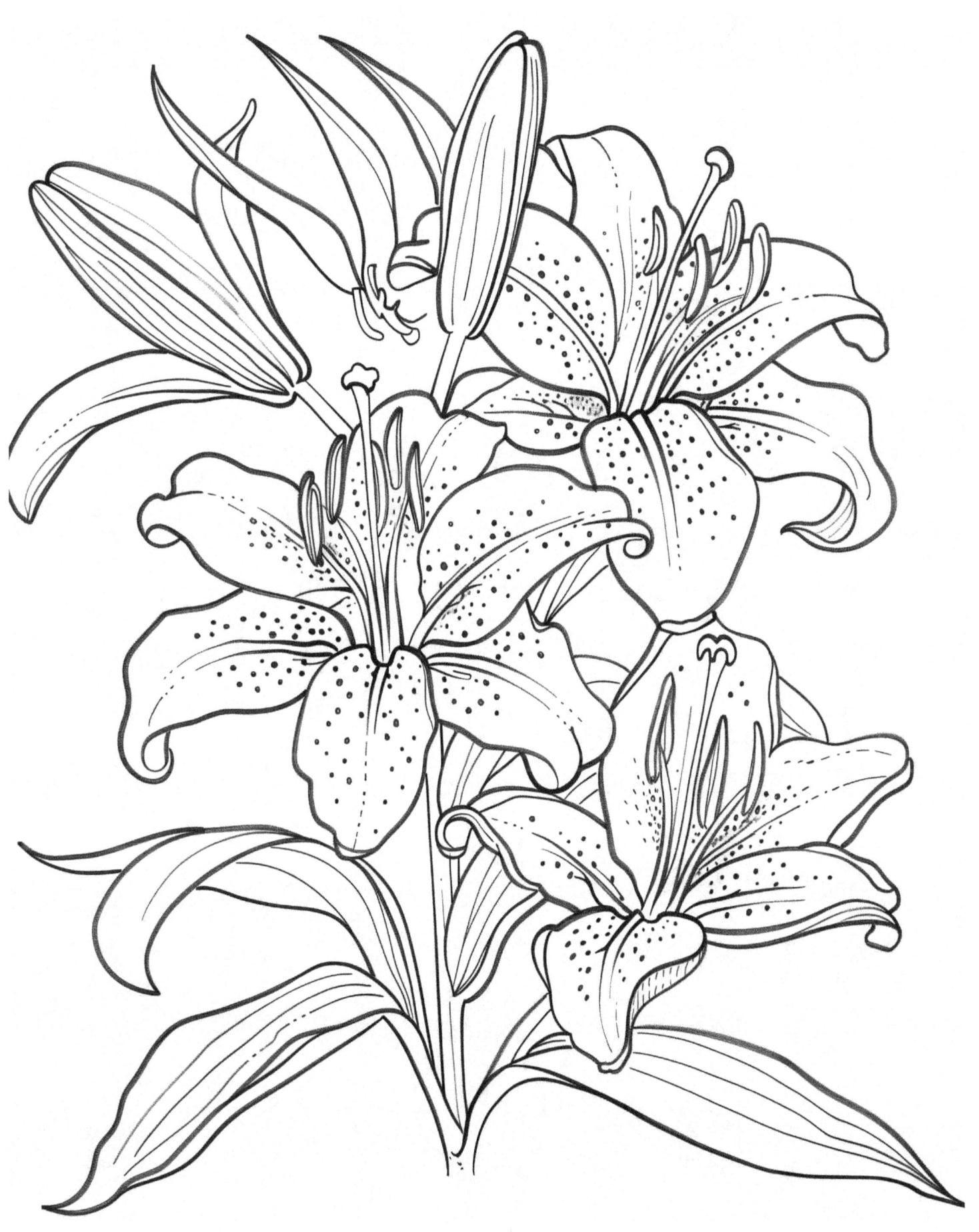

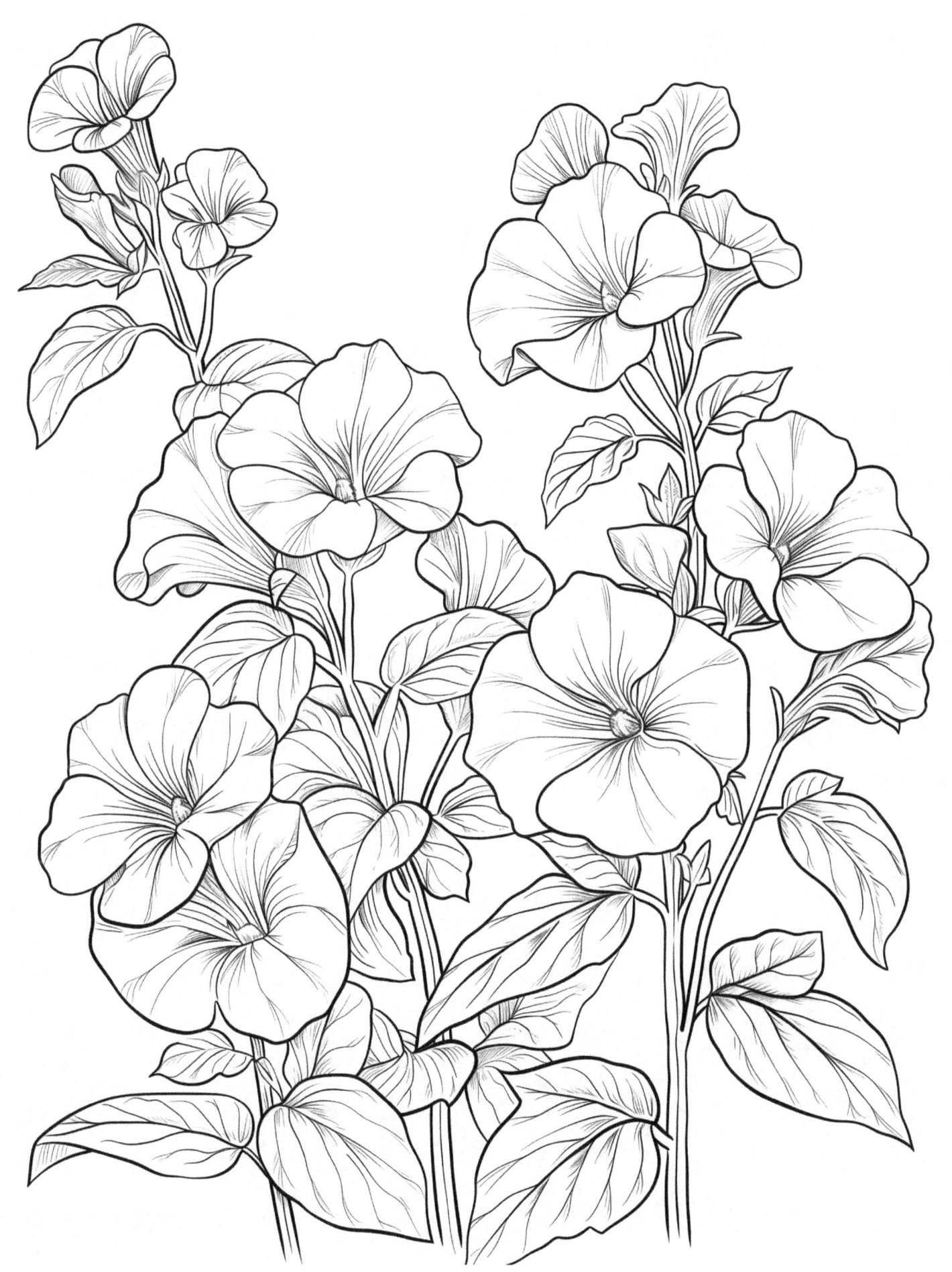

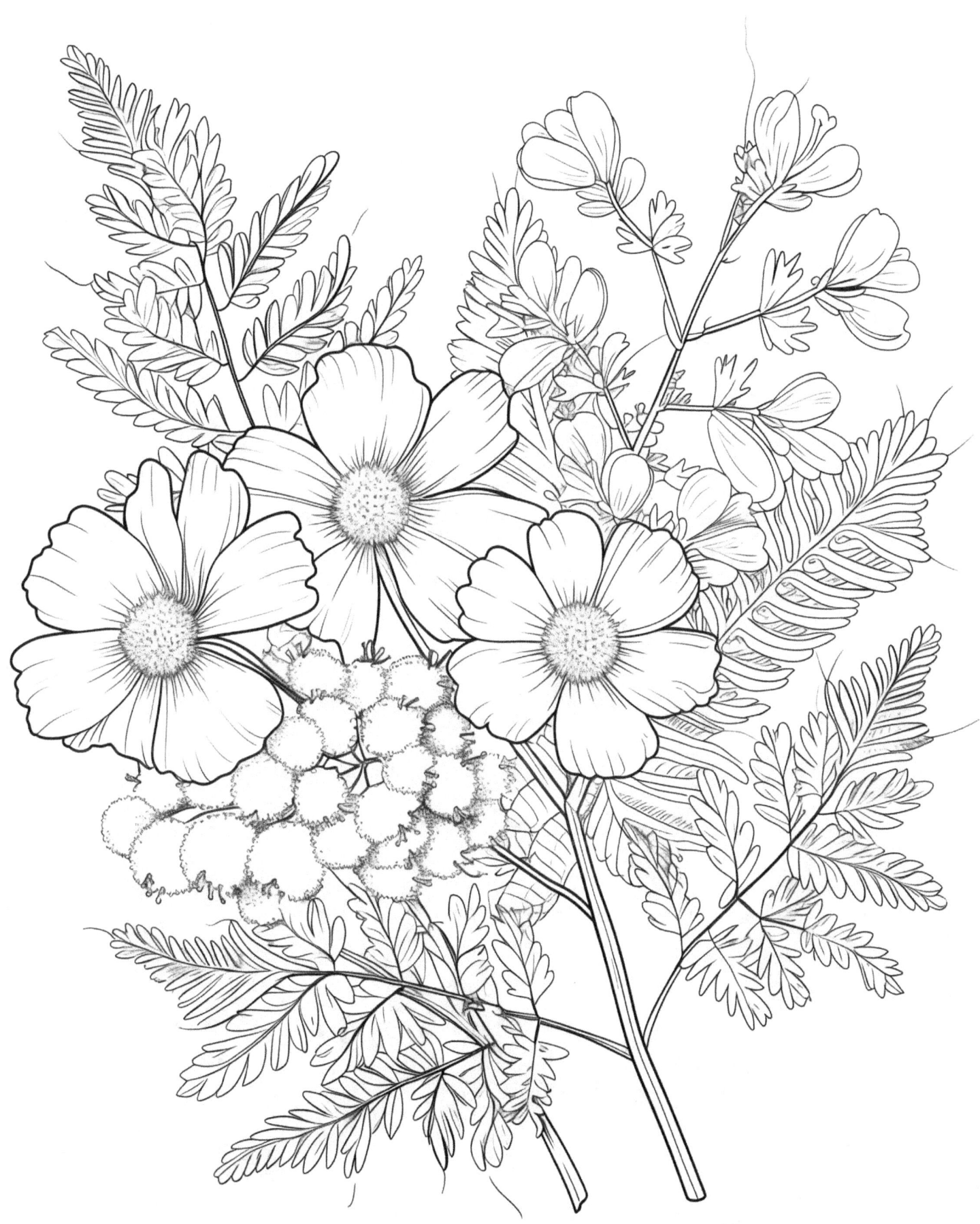

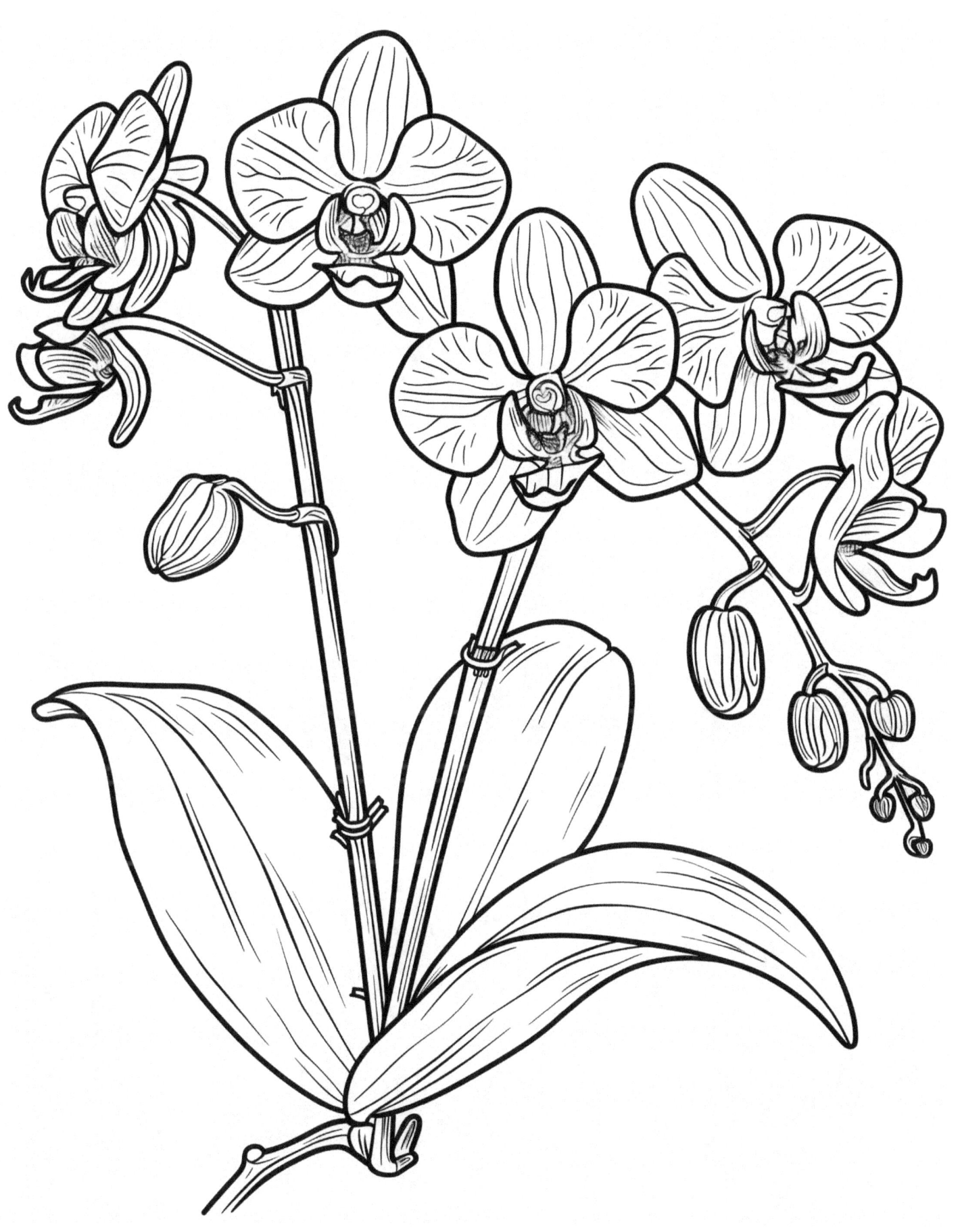

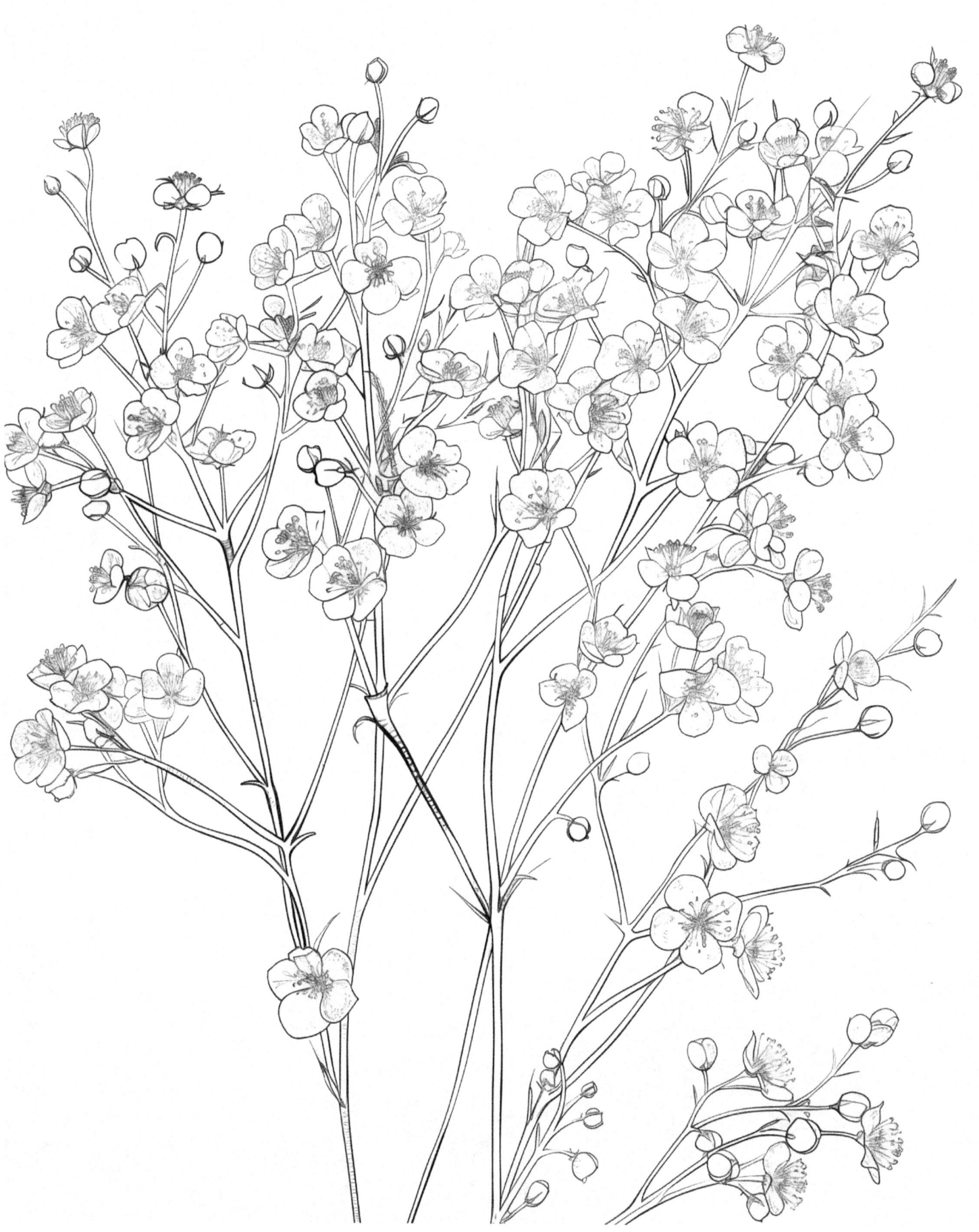

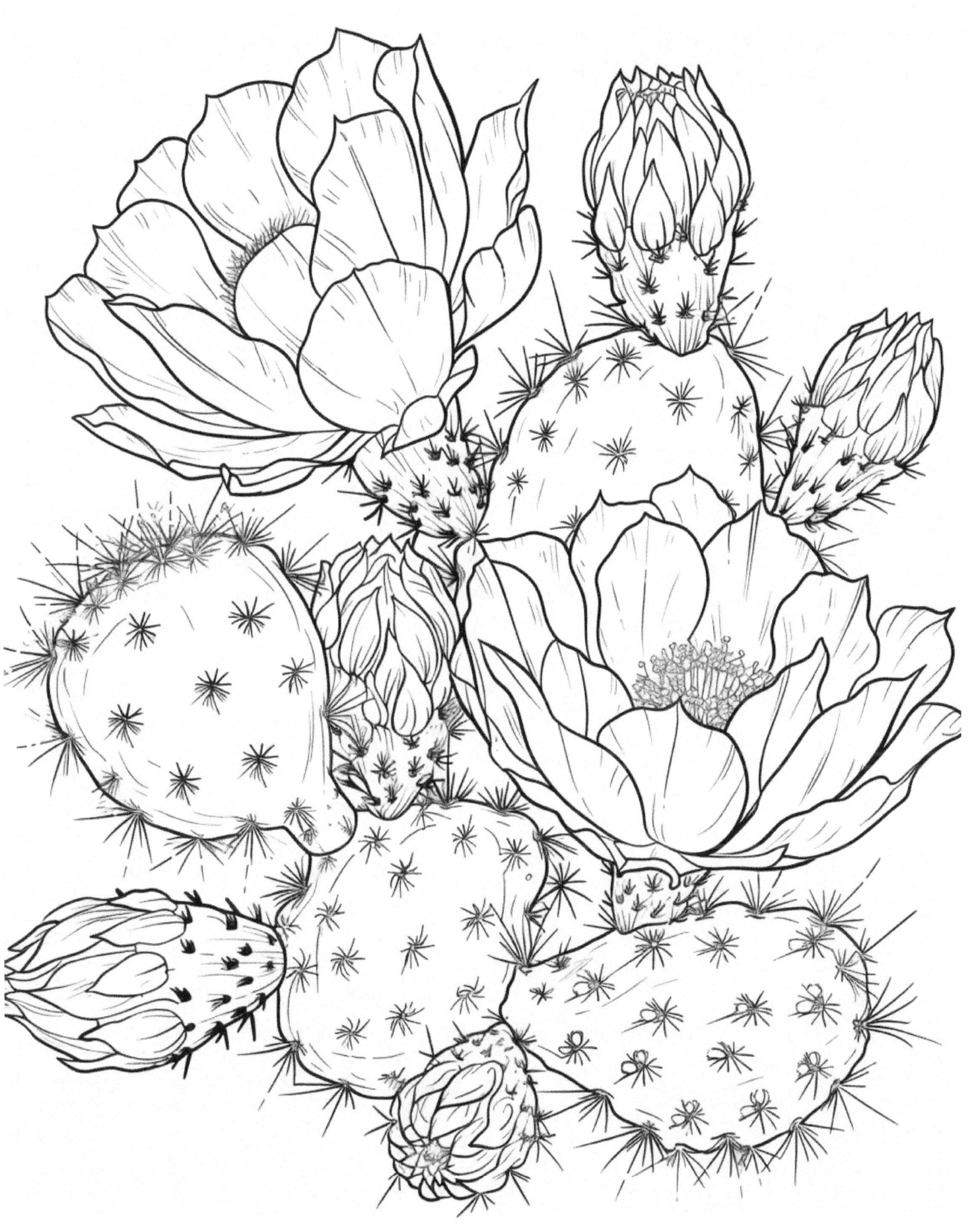

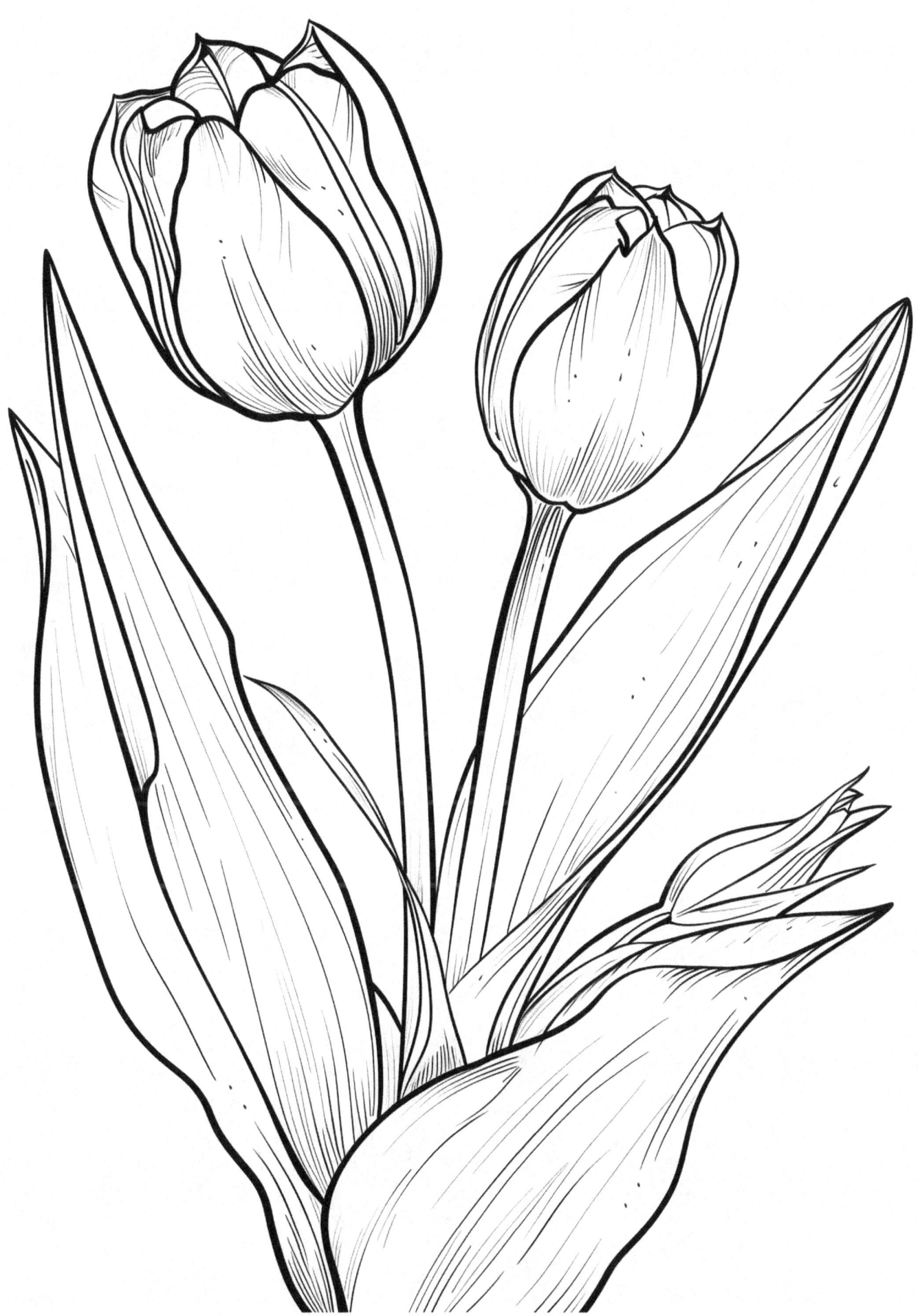

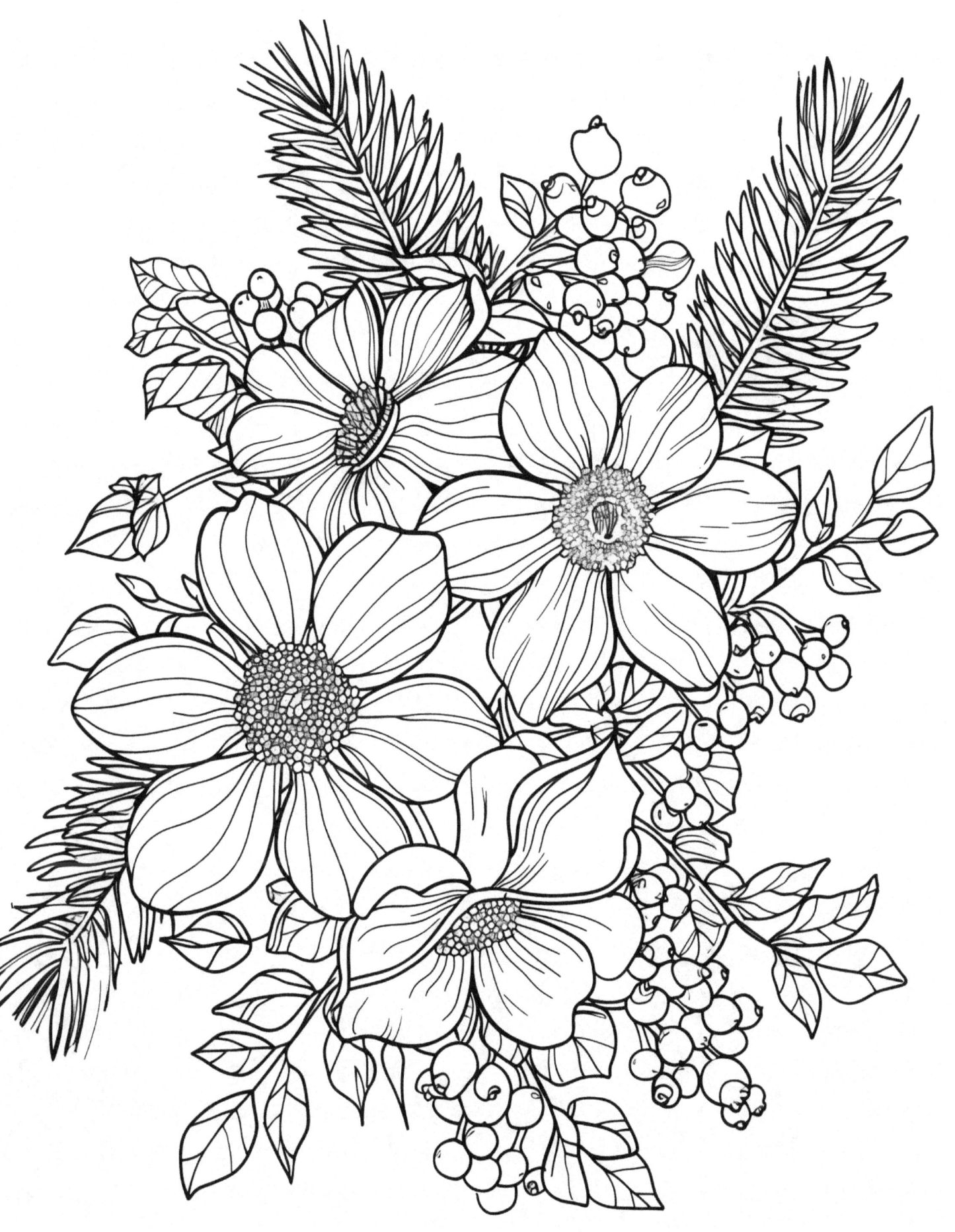

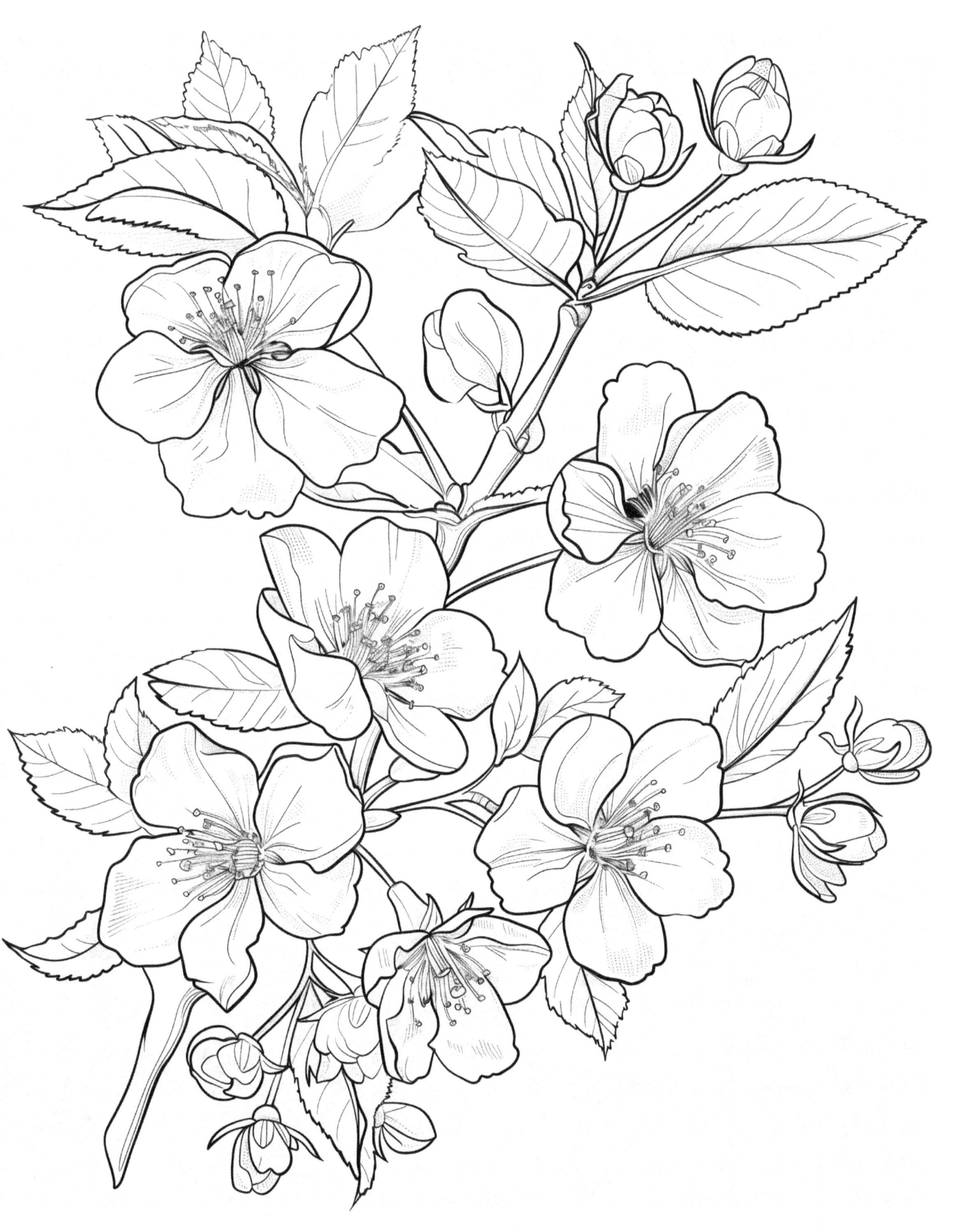

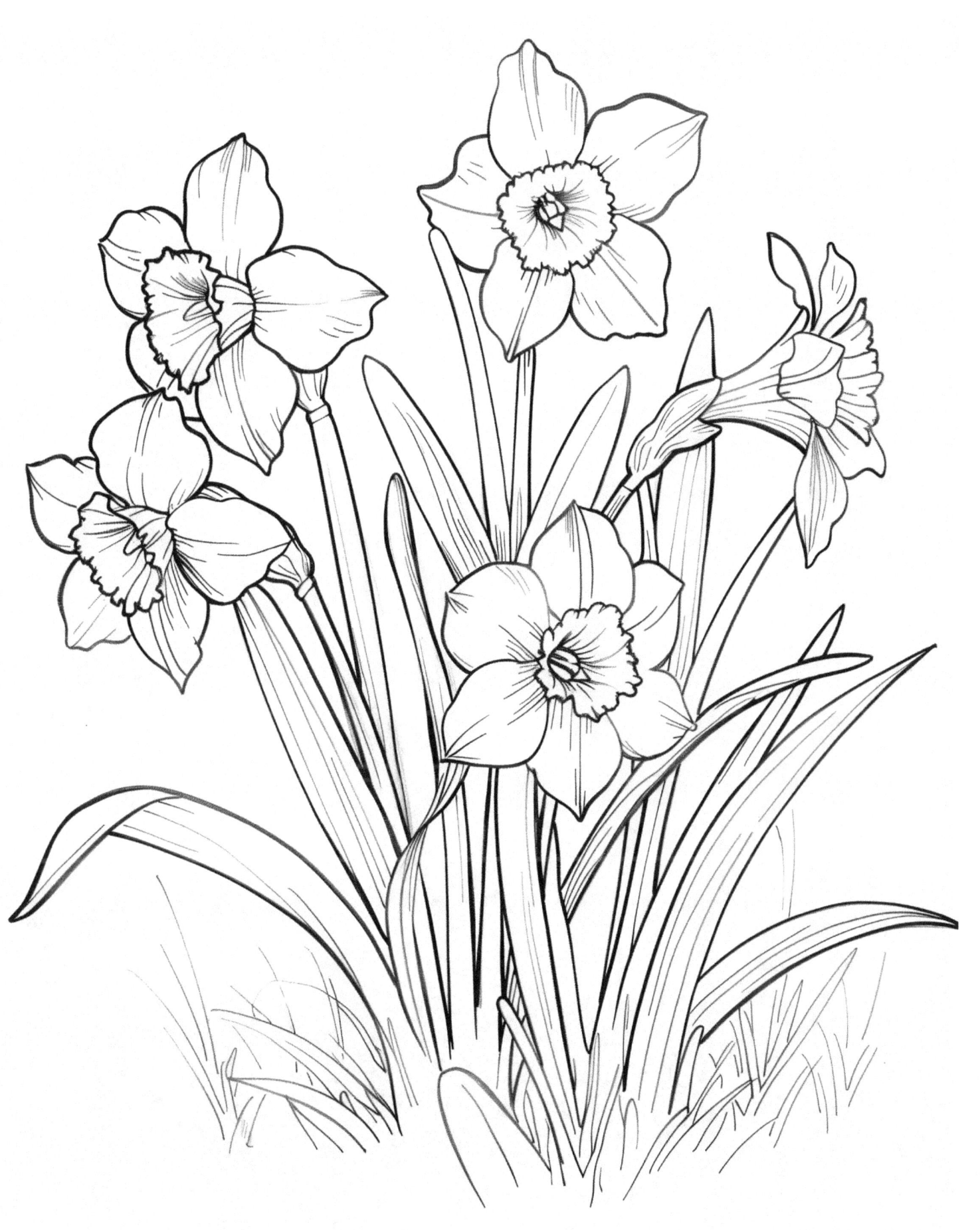

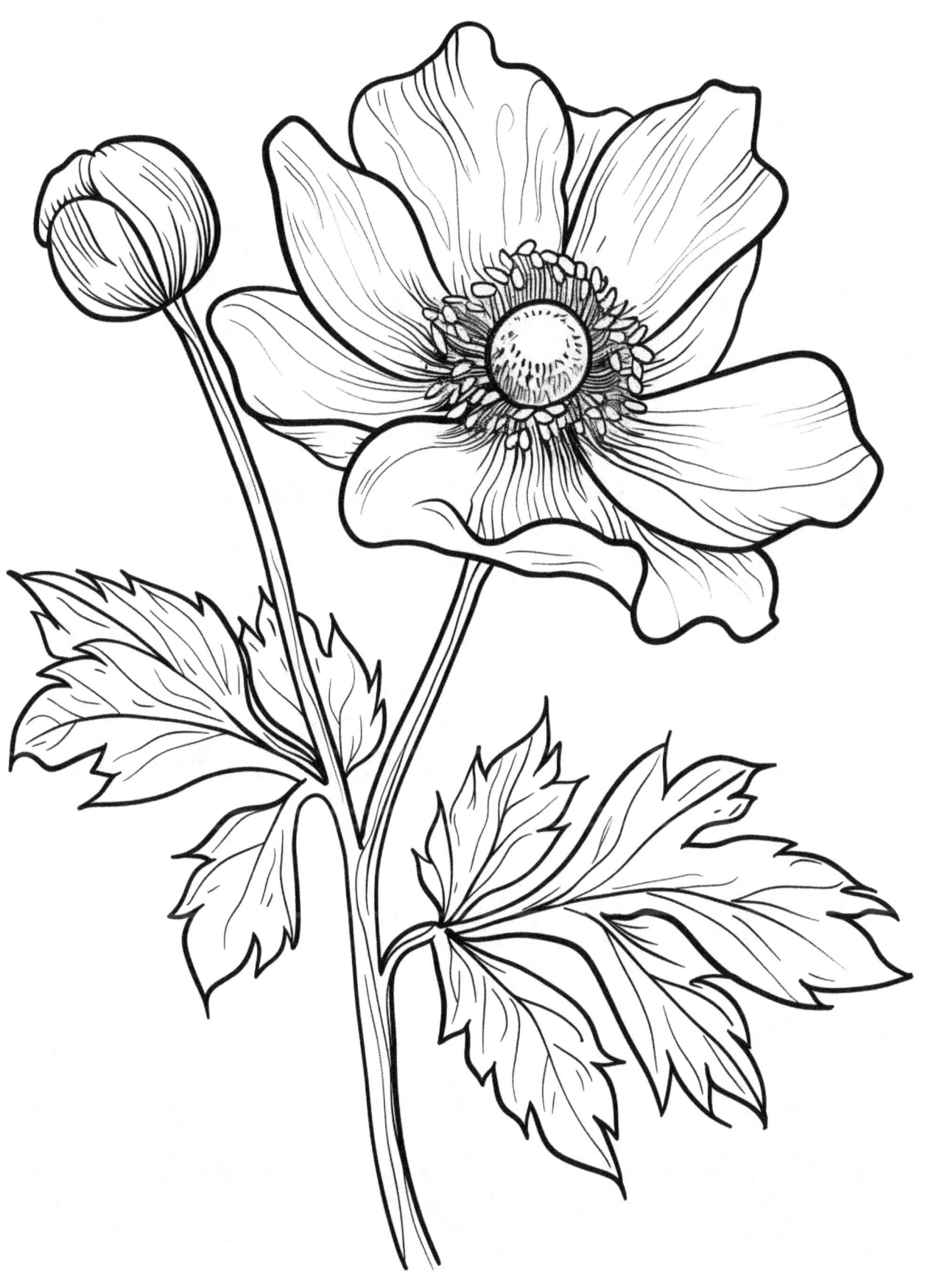

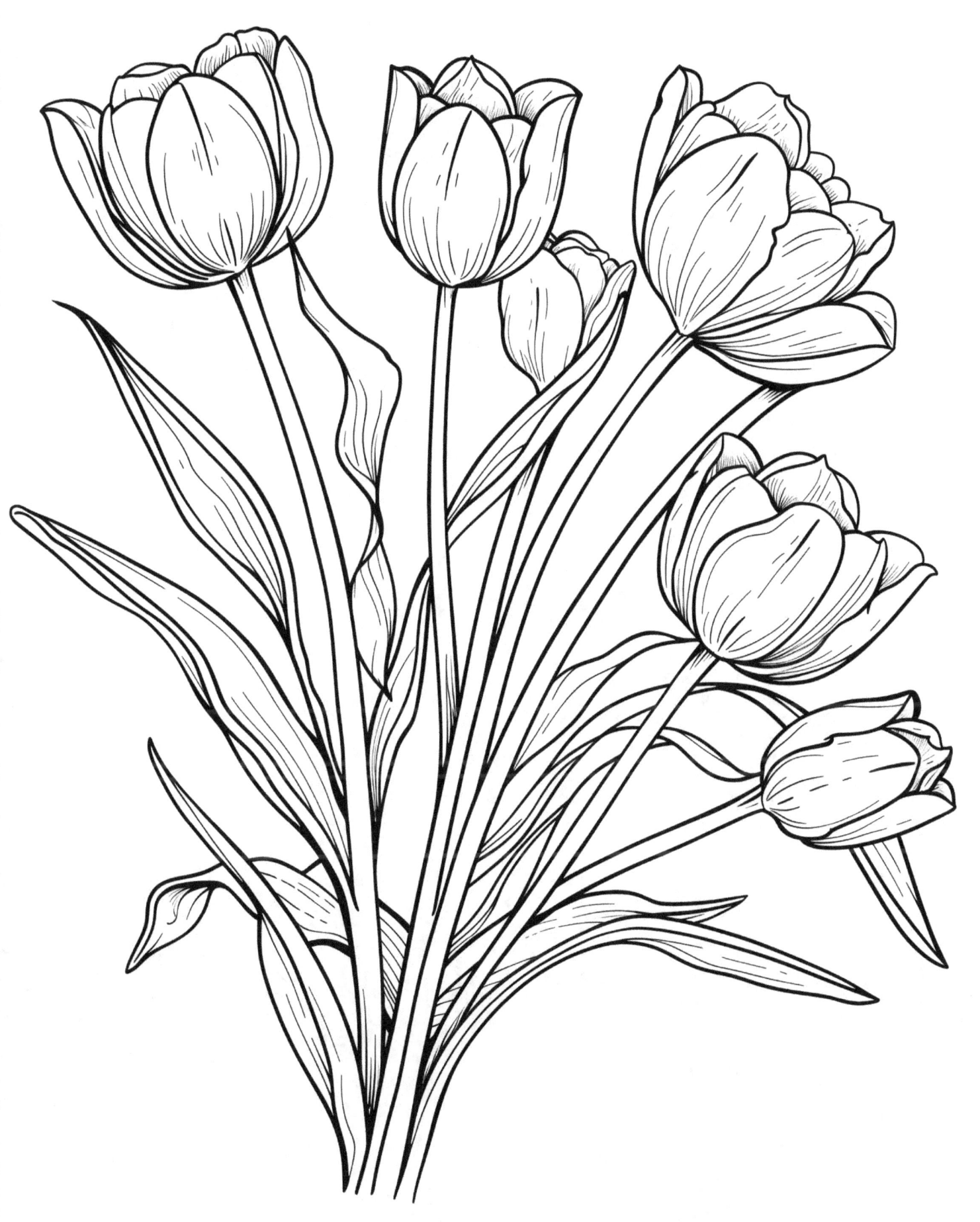

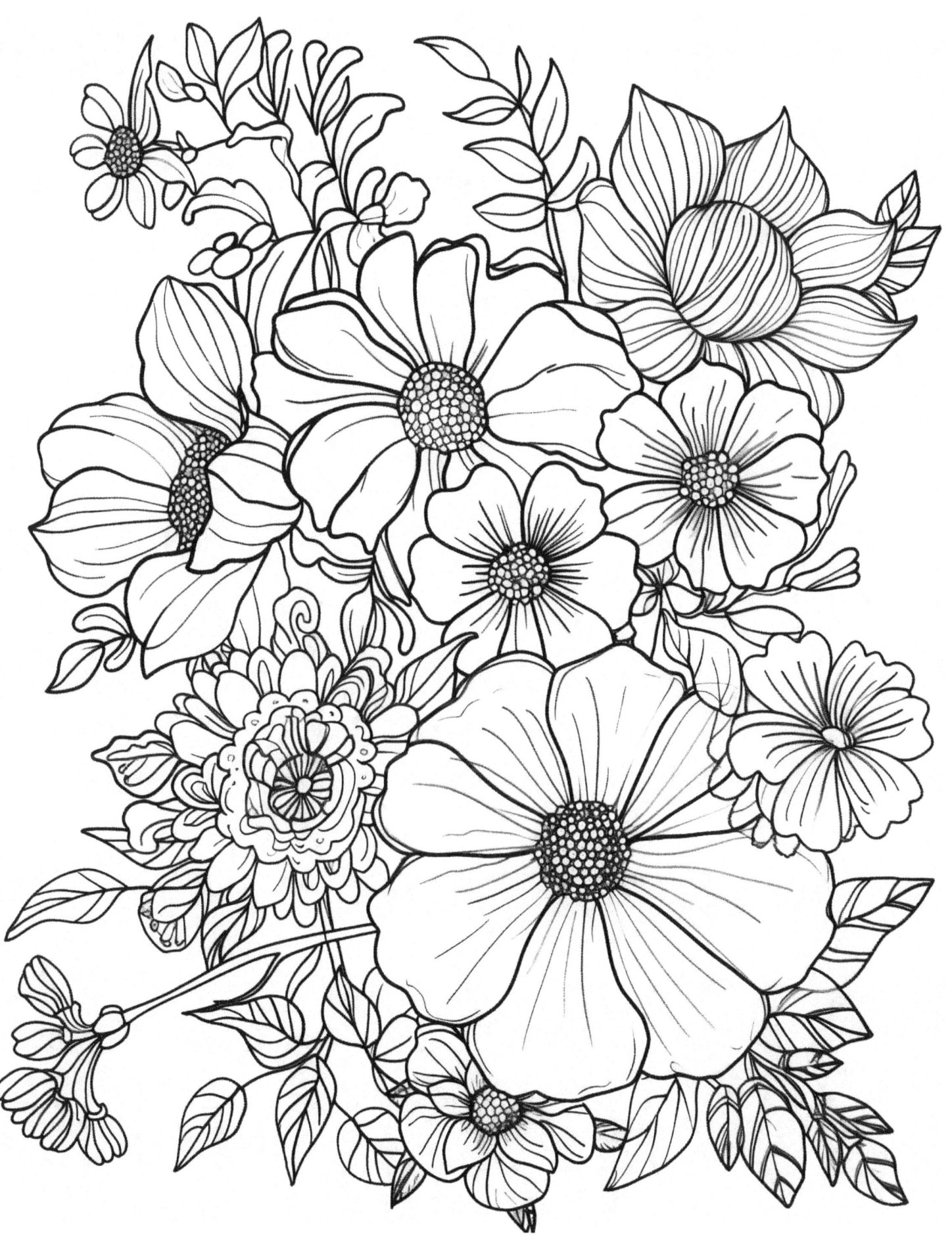

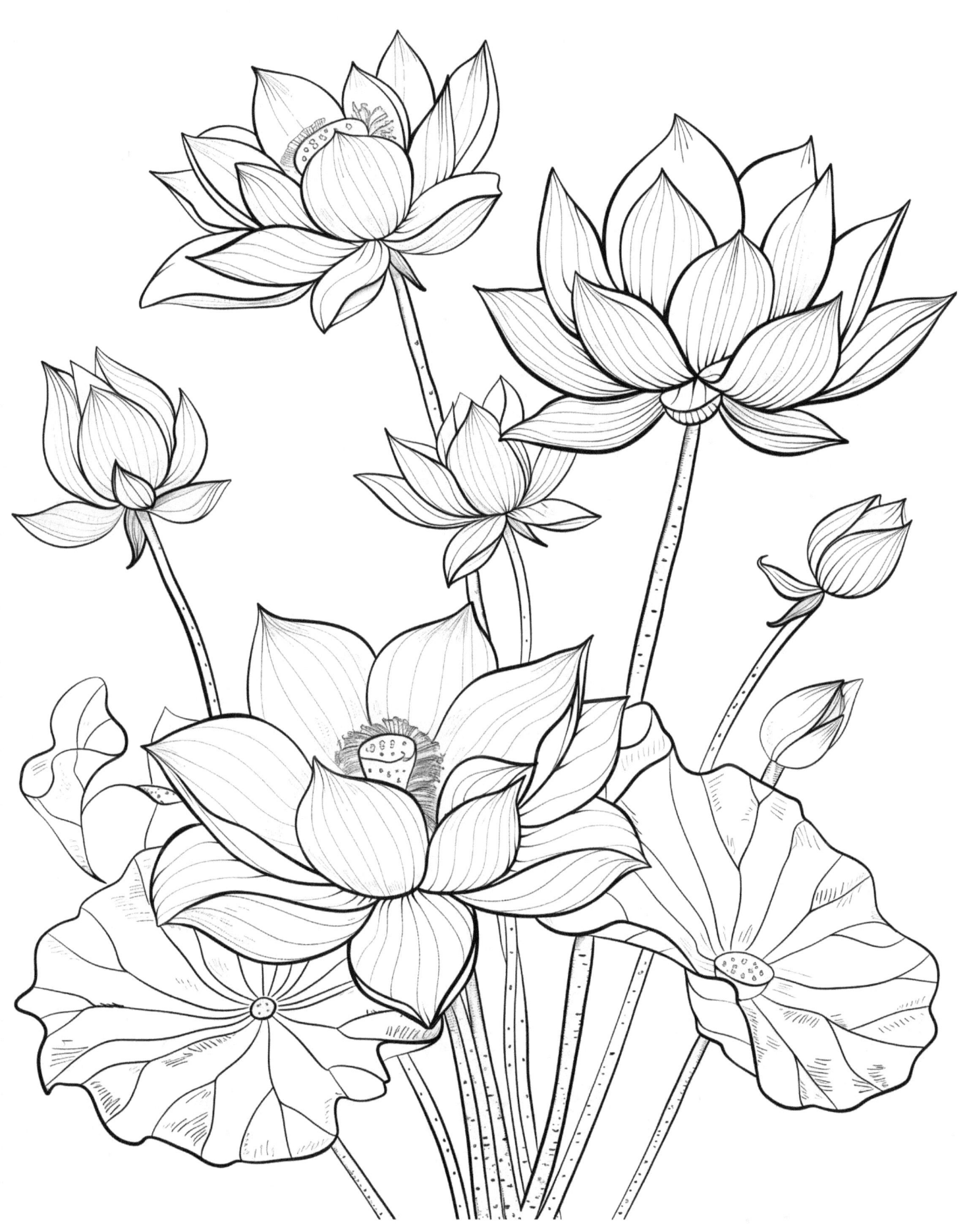

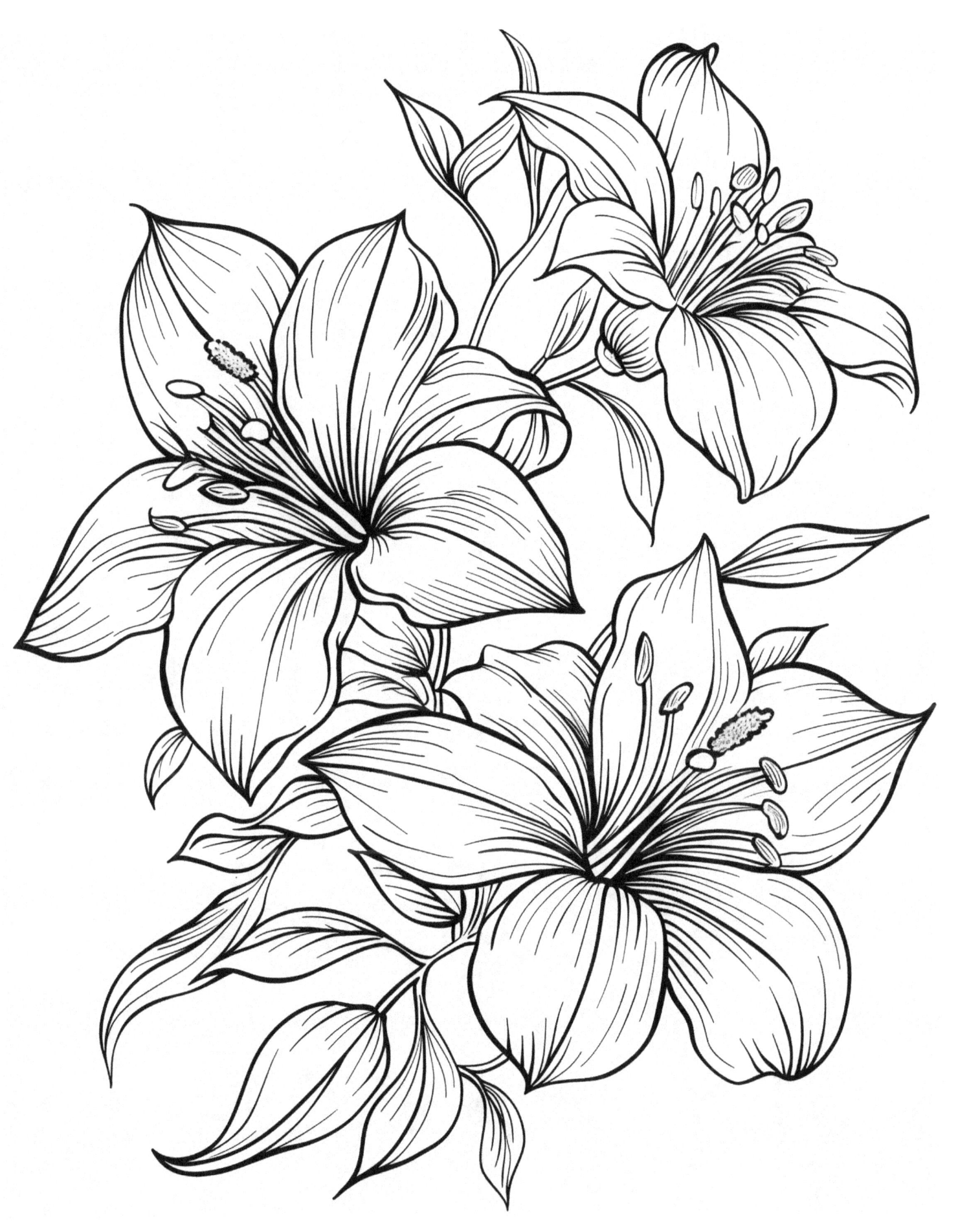

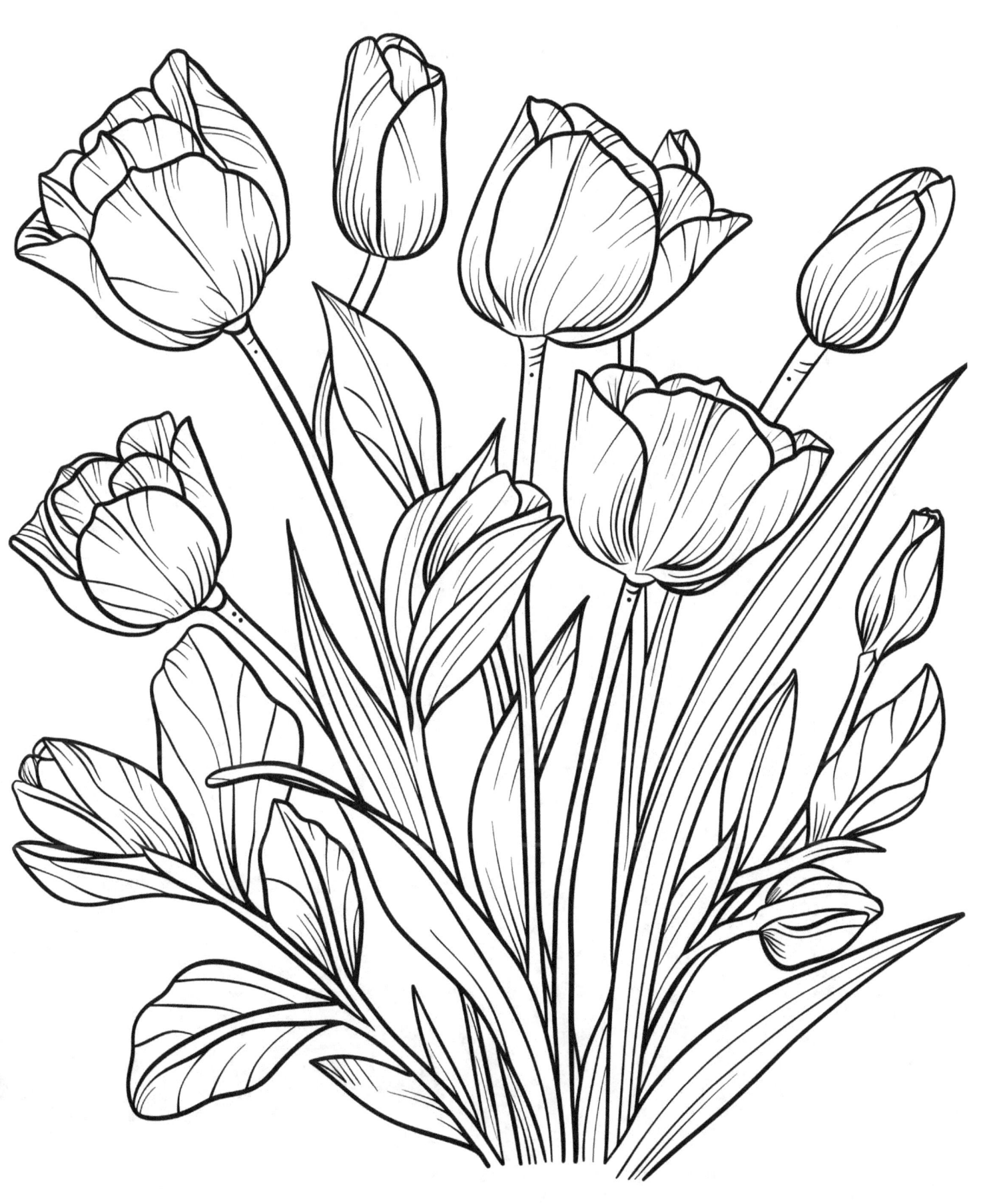

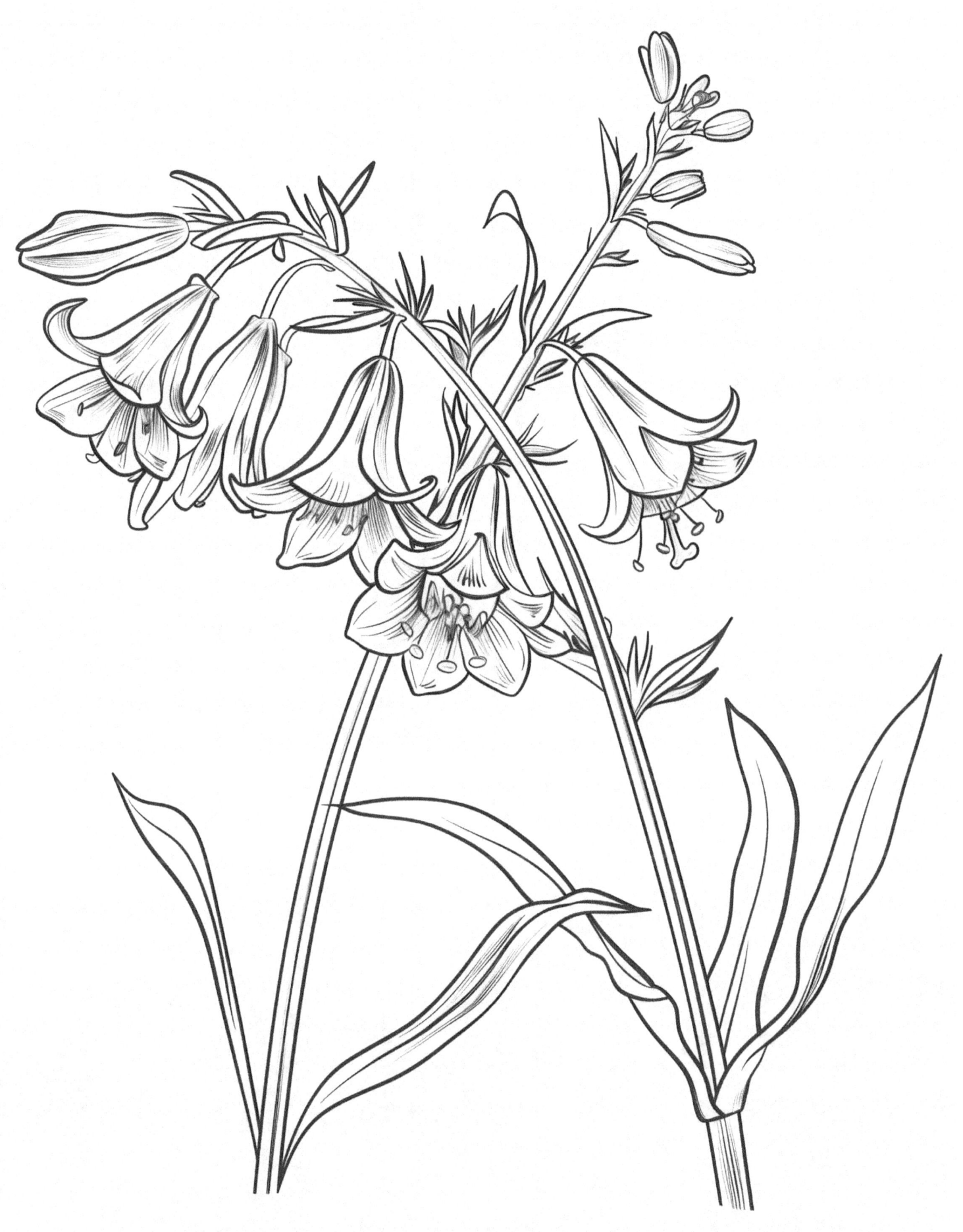

Copyright © 2024 by Talia Parsons
All rights reserved. No part of this publication may be reproduced or used in any form or by any meansgraphic, electronic, or mechanical, including photocopying, recording, or information storage-and-retrieval systems - without permission of the publisher.

www.ingramcontent.com/pod-product-compliance
Lightning Source LLC
Chambersburg PA
CBHW082354220526
45470CB00008B/2740